THE
Eyes
OF Midnight

To Howard
an inspiration
to ME!
Robert Wilson

THE
Eyes
OF Midnight

A Time of Terror in East Tennessee

BY ROBERT WILSON
with Richard Way

ARCHWAY
PUBLISHING

Archway Publishing books may be ordered through booksellers or by contacting:

Archway Publishing
1663 Liberty Drive
Bloomington, IN 47403
www.archwaypublishing.com
1 (888) 242-5904

ISBN: 978-1-4808-2593-2 (sc)
ISBN: 978-1-4808-2594-9 (e)

Library of Congress Control Number: 2015920942

Print information available on the last page.

Archway Publishing rev. date: 3/22/2016

For Sally,
my love, my strength

"At his best, man is the noblest of all animals; separated from law and justice he is the worst."
—Aristotle

With thanks to Richard Way
for his cooperation and support.

CONTENTS

Foreword xiii

Preface...xvii

Chapter 1   Harlots and Hickory Sticks....................................1

Chapter 2   Sworn Allegiance..8

Chapter 3   The Breedens: Blood Kin.................................... 16

Chapter 4   A Rising Opposition 22

Chapter 5   Forewarned But Not Forearmed..........................28

Chapter 6   Skirmish at Henderson Springs 33

Chapter 7   Turning Point 41

Chapter 8   Trial and Tribulation.. 47

Chapter 9   Bill and Laura 56

Chapter 10 Vengeance Beyond Measure................................63

Chapter 11 Death in the Night 70

Chapter 12 Captured and Cuffed...77

Chapter 13 New Law, New Judge 85

Chapter 14 Going Courting 92

Chapter 15 Insurrection Looms.. 100

Chapter 16 Last Steps 108

Epilogue 115

Acknowledgments... 123

Index... 127

FOREWORD

For generations a hush has shrouded the mystery of the "White Caps" of Sevier County. As deliverers of moralism through their own brand of vigilantism, this secret society eventually trampled the bounds of propriety—meeting their ultimate demise at the hands of the "Blue Bills" and Sheriff Tom Davis. Although the real story may never be known, *The Eyes of Midnight* sheds light on a time many families in our community would just as soon forget.

As a boy, I learned that sometime before the turn of the 20th century, a man by the name of Bob Catlett, who had married Mary Ann Wade, became a leader within the White Cap organization, and that Robert Ira (Bob) Wade, his young, unmarried brother-in-law, was somehow involved in their activities. In 1899, the hangings of Catlett Tipton and Pleas Wynn for the murders of Bill and Laura Whaley marked the end of the White Cap era. Five years later, Bob Wade married Victoria Atchley Wade, a union that produced a daughter, Anna, in 1905, and a son, Dwight, in 1907. Not long after, Bob and Victoria separated and later divorced. Bob Wade remarried, moved to Blount County, and died an early death in 1921. Anna, a teacher and businesswoman, married and moved to Anderson County. Dwight Wade wed in 1939 and had four sons, including yours truly. Because all of "the boys" were born between 1940 and 1949, none of us, of course, could have known our grandfather. My impression has always been that my father and Aunt Anna, although proud of the Wade name, had few recollections of their short time together as a traditional family. In consequence, family lore offered little information about the White Caps. It was not until 1973, when I began to practice law in an office next to the Sevier County Courthouse—only a few feet from where the Tipton/Wynn scaffolds once stood—that I began to hear more details about this hooded band, their original purpose, and the disgraceful end of their reign.

I specifically recall a conversation in the early 1980's with then State Senator Victor Ashe (most recently Ambassador to Poland), who practiced law for a time in Knoxville before becoming the city's mayor. Victor and I exchanged the information he had about his grandfather, Dr. James Henderson, a courageous Blue Bill who was shot and killed during the White Cap era, and what little I knew of my grandfather Wade. Those conversations sparked my interest. I first read a reprint of Crozier's 1899 rendition of the White Cap story, then the Cas Walker publication—which appeared to be more fable than fact, and, importantly, listened to some of the "old-timers' " tales. Years passed, however, before the late "Professor" Don Paine, the state's preeminent lawyer-historian meticulously researched the trial records of Tipton, Wynn, and Bob Catlett—all the way to the Tennessee Supreme Court. He learned that Bob Wade had been indicted as an accessory during the White Cap era but never tried, the state having eventually dismissed the charges—for reasons lost forever. Ironically, by the time Don Paine completed his studies, I served as a member of that Supreme Court—appointed to the office over a hundred years after the eventual acquittal of Bob Catlett for his alleged role in the Whaley murders. On two memorable occasions, Don and I reviewed the court documents he had found in our Court's archives. I never missed an opportunity to hear him speak on the subject, and, when he did, he was a model of diplomacy—careful not to tarnish the reputations of White Cap descendants.

Resurrecting history after 120 years is no easy task. The surnames of many of the Sevier Countians identified in *The Eyes of Midnight* exist today. The McMahans, Mapleses, Davises, Wynns, Catletts, and Whaleys are among our most prominent citizens. Kith and kin of the White Caps survive, but few know the particulars of the 1890s—time, secrecy, and, yes, even shame and regret, may cloud the recollections of what really happened during those years—before the rule of law laid the groundwork for what is today a proud and prosperous community.

Gary R. Wade
Vice President and Dean
Lincoln Memorial University
Duncan School of Law
Former Chief Justice,
Tennessee Supreme Court

PREFACE

Sometimes the truth can have a pretty ugly face.

That being the case, there are many who choose not to look at it any more than necessary. In America, slavery has that kind of face, as do the lynchings, violence, and intimidation that followed its abolition. So do certain acts of wartime and terrorism.

And so does one decade in the history of a single, bucolic little county in East Tennessee.

Even 120 years later, there are still those in Sevier County—longtime residents—who have only a broken knowledge of the decade that was defined by a large and lawless band known as the White Caps. Others would just as soon not talk about it even today.

Before it became one of Tennessee tourism's crown jewels, Sevier County was a sedate place, dotted with family farms, crystal streams, and green pristine mountains. Its heritage was one of cultural establishment and migration, not based on some significant war battle or a cataclysmic natural disaster. It was just a quiet little county, carved out of the larger Jefferson County to the north, and named for the first governor of the state, John Sevier, a political and military leader and a member of Congress. The people of Sevier County tended to settle where people the world over have always done so—near a source of clean water—and to do what they had to do to survive.

With the exception of the tumultuous Civil War years, life flowed peacefully along in that manner for a hundred years, from the founding of the state in 1796 until just before the 1900s began. It was then that the county fell into a shadow of fear and uncertainty that few at that time talked openly about. That reluctance took decades to fade away, although there are still some whose sense of family dictates that the whole period be forgotten. But the White Cap era is, in modern parlance, really a thing.

However, many who have lived in the region, even for decades, are unaware of this slice of history. Early on that was because to chronicle the actions of the White Caps would have endangered a person's good health or life expectancy. Thus, the only first-hand accounts we have in the twenty-first century are in one thin volume written in real time and produced by Ethelred W. Crozier, who census records list as publisher of the City Directory in Knoxville. His work was titled *The White Caps: A History of the Organization in Sevier County*, published in 1899.

Now, print journalists all over the nation have for years accepted the City Directory in any given metropolitan area as a reliable source for names, residences, businesses, phone numbers, and more. Before the Internet, the City Directory was just about the only way to look up who lived at a particular address or whose was a certain phone number. So the reputation of its publisher for accuracy in any city was generally accepted. There is no reason to believe Crozier was any less attentive to accuracy than any of his colleagues elsewhere.

There is no author listed on the cover of *The White Caps*. To be identified as the one who wrote the words in that book at that time could have gotten a man a visit from the very vigilantes he was writing about. Still, it remains the closest thing we have to an eyewitness account.

The Eyes of Midnight is not just a "rewrite" of Crozier's book. Additional detail has been added from multiple sources to provide as complete a retelling of the White Cap story as possible. Beyond question, there are holes in the narrative—doubtless some that will never be filled. But it is as true, accurate, and complete as possible.

The reader who looks for all the ragged edges of a story to be neatly hemmed and trimmed or who simply has a strong sense of justice may well be disappointed in how this story ends. But that's the way history is sometimes.

As a retired journalist, I place great importance on truth and accuracy, and the process of pulling this story together from multiple—sometimes conflicting—sources was at times frustrating and required judgment calls on my part as to what was likely the more trustworthy information based on the source. For instance, if the Crozier account listed one date for the death of an individual but that person's gravestone indicated another, I went with the one that somebody carved into a hunk of granite, believing that an act of craftsmanship and permanency, performed as the event happened, was probably more accurate than a retelling of the event based on someone's memory.

Furthermore, I decided early on that to approach this narrative as a heavily footnoted work of scholarship might compromise the drama, suspense, and emotion that is naturally woven through it. Footnotes would have interrupted the flow, I believe, eroding the intensity of the story without adding anything back that would justify their existence.

Information sources for *The Eyes of Midnight* are acknowledged at the end of the book. That will satisfy a journalist's natural inclination to reveal to his reader where he got his information. However, when it comes to delving into the thought processes of the characters involved—and they are all real people—I have taken some minimal measure of license, believing that it is not out of bounds for a thinking person to infer what those thoughts might have been based on what was going on around them at the time.

Spoken quotes, though, have been reproduced verbatim, but in the full knowledge that they may have undergone some modification by memory before they got to me. Obviously, no one alive today has firsthand knowledge of the events chronicled in this volume. Any verbal accounts or anecdotal information from a living individual would be at least two generations removed—probably more—from the actual occurrence and becomes, to a journalist, less reliable as absolute truth with each step.

That aspect of my work is exaggerated by the fact that for at least a couple of generations after the White Cap era, almost nobody was inclined to talk about it openly outside their own family. Indeed, for a few decades into the twentieth century, the statutes of limitation on some of these events had still not run out. Some expired only when the people involved died.

That is why the Crozier book has remained, until now, the closest thing Sevier County has had to a comprehensive compendium on the White Cap story. And Crozier's book was published before the climactic event actually occurred. Crozier's book was probably typeset by hand, because the first Merganthaler Linotype mechanical typesetters were produced only a couple of years before the White Cap era began and, in all likelihood, had not found their way into East Tennessee by then.

The White Cap period is a fascinating slice of American and Sevier County history that has long deserved a deeper and broader examination. *The Eyes of Midnight* is intended to be exactly that.

CHAPTER ONE

Harlots and Hickory Sticks

How could it come to this?" Sheriff Tom Davis thought as he surveyed the small crowd around him, sweltering in an East Tennessee July.

Seven years of beatings and bullets, fear and treachery, unspeakable cruelty visited by neighbor upon neighbor. And this is the result: more death.

The difference this time, Davis thought, is that these two men need to die. Almost no one in the crowd would dispute that. What *these* men did even God could not forgive. Neither could the state of Tennessee.

Davis and a handful of others were crowded onto a wooden platform that creaked beneath its load as the scene played out. A few steps away from Davis stood two of his childhood pals, talking in hushed voices to family members and ministers. Prayers for forgiveness rose through the cloudy gloom to a God with more mercy—the condemned hoped—than they had themselves demonstrated.

Davis observed that the men were strikingly calm. Occasionally they glanced at the ropes, carefully knotted with nooses at one end and Eternity at the other. And they talked in whispers to their women, who would shortly be widowed by court order. At the court's instruction, the gallows had been enclosed inside a high, stockade-like fence to provide some level of privacy to a legal proceeding that would prove to be the last of its kind in Sevier County. It was 1899.

Just short of a hundred people were allowed inside the enclosure, most of them family members, officers of the law, clergymen, lawyers, and newspapermen. It was crowded, and it was hot, made all the more uncomfortable by Victorian-era fashions that dictated proper women be covered from neck to shoe top and men wear string ties, heavy coats, and trousers regardless of prevailing temperatures. Outside the fence, hundreds more milled about the courthouse lawn, their presence and numbers a testament to the significance of this event.

Sheriff Davis stood silent and stone faced on a corner of the platform. He had willingly assumed the position he now held, and he had done so for all the right reasons. He had known all along that the job might require him to preside over such a proceeding. Still, when it came right down to intentionally taking people's lives— even with all the legalities adhered to—it had turned out to be more uncomfortable than Davis expected.

"How could it come to this?" The question kept coming back like the words to a song you cannot put out of your head.

How could the fabric of a rural county like Sevier get ripped and twisted and torn almost instantly into a place where people were held hostage by the night. Where even doors locked at sundown offered little protection from...well, you never knew who.

Sevier County had been a place where people mostly kept to themselves, taking care of their own business and letting others take care of theirs. The long Tennessee summers allowed them to grow what they needed: wheat, corn, and vegetables or hay for the livestock. That was in the northern and western parts of the county.

In the eastern and southern sections, forested mountains rose above the flatlands. The folds and hollows of the hills were home to only the most hardy—and they were content with only minimal contact with others. There they hunted the woods, made their home-brew whiskey, and scratched an existence out of a terrain not much suited for agriculture. The sun's morning arrival came a little later here, because it had to rise over a hilltop before permeating the deep forest. To live there you had to be tougher'n the nose on a red-headed peckerwood and near 'bout as hard headed.

Even so, just a few years prior, the serenity of this county was most often broken only by the church bells on Sunday morning. Neighbors, if you had any, supported each other with a hot meal or a load of firewood for a shut-in down the road. When necessary, they would even help each other dig a well or a grave.

Outsiders...well, they usually got a sideways eyeballing. If you didn't know somebody's daddy or his sister or you weren't his cousin a couple of times removed, then some amount of suspicion was a perfectly logical first reaction. *For everyone.*

It was a community of 22,000 souls who had yet to take their first spin around the Industrial Revolution. Human advancement came a little later to such places.

But in 1892 there arrived a dark, new culture, faceless and

without compassion. It rolled with a mob's momentum and seemed to gain strength and vitality through collective evil. It traveled the dirt roads and canopied footpaths to wherever it decided something needed fixing or a lesson needed to be taught. And it carried out its wicked justice in a most hideous fashion, as often as not on those least able to resist.

They called themselves White Caps. It was a name that just a few years later would not be spoken so much as it would be spat into the Sevier County dust.

Exactly how the White Caps initially came to exist seems lost to history; accounts vary. The most authoritative ones, those compiled during the actual events, do not really offer much of a clue. This is not surprising, since publishing that kind of detail contemporaneously could mean getting one's body perforated in a 12-gauge sort of a way.

Indeed, White Capping was a subject best left alone in Sevier County well into the second half of the twentieth century, because first-generation descendants of those involved were still alive and still touchy about having Pappy's legacy stained with lawlessness. That probably also accounts for the scarcity of any cohesive chronicle of the White Cap phenomenon.

One source traces the White Caps' formation to an offhand remark made by a judge at a café luncheon in Sevierville, the county seat. The judge had lamented that he could not get convictions against a half-dozen or so unnamed women who had apparently migrated from Knoxville and established a whorehouse in Emert's Cove. Industrialization had not made it to the Sevier County backcountry, but the world's oldest profession had.

The morals charge on which the convictions were being sought was lewdness, which in that era was code for fornication and adultery.

But the judge is said to have told his luncheon companions that the women always evaded charges or defeated conviction because witnesses—presumably the men who had patronized the business—would lie under oath, saying they had not been there. And because of the private nature of this commercial enterprise, their testimony was difficult-if not-impossible to refute. Furthermore, the men had additional motivation to absolve the women of culpability so that they would not have to return home to a profoundly pissed off wifemate should they testify for the prosecution.

One of the judge's lunch partners is alleged to have suggested that a band of men be formed to go to Copeland Creek and give the women a whipping and instructions to leave the county or face additional—and more stern—retribution.

There is no hard evidence that this was the start of White Capping in Sevier County. Only hearsay. Just as impossible to confirm is the other account of the White Cap formation.

No transcript of the statement has been found, but it is also said that a judge made a similar suggestion in open court, supposedly following a charge to a just-seated grand jury.

"Gentlemen," the judge is alleged to have said, "we bring these women in from Copeland Creek (not too far from Emert's Cove) and charge them with lewdness. But men who forsake their wives always come in and swear them out, lying to get an acquittal."

He then suggested some of them band together, disguise themselves with hoods and bed sheets and go to Copeland Creek to whip the women until they "straighten up and be the kind of women they should be. They are a disgrace to the community."

Historically accurate? Unknown and presumably unknowable. In any case, either scenario represents a judicial foul ball of immense proportions, if not downright conspiracy.

Irrespective, the raid did happen.

In 1892 the wayward women of Copeland Creek woke one morning to find a bundle of hickory switches —also called withes— on their front steps. Attached was a note that advised them to leave the community or face a whipping with the withes. It was signed by the "White Caps." In either defiance or disbelief, the women remained.

But the White Caps were dead serious and shortly made good on their threat, and the women got a thrashing. The White Caps left them with another warning that failure to flee would result in another, even more brutal beating. Having been made believers, the women retreated to Knoxville where their potential customer base was greater, even if the competition for their product was, too.

And so it started, demonstrating that the road that leads to the moral high ground sometimes runs through the valley of the shadow of lawlessness.

Without a doubt the Copeland Creek whores were on the south side of the law and imminently short of the glory by community standards. On the other hand, the White Cap response—irrespective of its moral righteousness—constituted assault, plain and simple. And it was entirely illegal.

The ends having been justified, though, a sense of amused approval spread through the cove, along with a confidence that other questionable behavior might be similarly modified. If it had stopped there, the story would be over. But it did not, and what started out as a fairly mild enforcement of Victorian values in an isolated, God-fearing community eventually degenerated into an unabated wave of crime with no moral underpinning whatsoever.

That is how it could come to this. Sheriff Davis knew all that, but still for it to lead to this moment with these people on this wooden platform was almost like a stage play.

The bell in the 130-foot tower of Sevier County's new courthouse had tolled 1:00. The platform had lost the greater measure of its load. Black hoods covered the faces of the condemned. It was time to hand two sinful souls over to God.

Davis's gaze rose from his boot tops to make eye contact with his deputy standing at the opposite corner with his hand on the trapdoor release.

Davis drew a jagged breath. And he nodded.

CHAPTER TWO
Sworn Allegiance

The Gilded Age did not bring much gold or anything else that glittered to Sevier County.

Industrialization was giving birth to a new class of American aristocracy as the nation was still trying to throw off the cloak of the Civil War and turn its attention to an expanding future. Former slaves and their children were still trying to determine their place in the social order, as were the ever-growing throngs of immigrants who came to America looking for freedom, jobs, and a prosperity that even internal armed conflict could not destroy.

Sevier County, though, had little that sparkled in the sun, aside from the morning dew on the mountaintops. Secluded and insular, the county was probably little aware of the exploding wealth and ostentatious excesses of the cities "up East." Little of that had reached as far south as Tennessee.

But in 1892 there was one notable exception. Biltmore, the palatial enterprise of George Washington Vanderbilt II, was half-built that year. Construction had begun 3 years before; completion would come 3 years after. Steamboats and railroads had brought Vanderbilt his money, and his money had brought Biltmore to a hilly section of North Carolina not unlike Sevier County in terrain and scenery.

Like much of East Tennessee, Sevier swam against the current during the Civil War. The loyalties of its residents were sharply divided, with some supporting Northern forces and others sympathizing with the Confederates. Slavery was not unknown to Sevier County, but affluence was confined to a very few, and only the wealthy could afford the luxury of owning other people. So Sevier was not entirely onboard as Tennessee and every other state around it tried to bail out of "a more perfect union" to join one that was markedly less so.

After the war, Sevier County was Republican down to its woolen socks, a place without enough Democrats for a decent game of cards. So as 1892 blossomed, the county was still a hardscrabble Appalachian enclave that depended much more on horses than it did on horsepower.

Elsewhere, it was a year that brought its share of innovation. James Naismith published the rules for basketball, a patent was sought for the Diesel engine, a corporate merger created General Electric, Thomas Edison got a patent for the telegraph, and Tchaikovsky premiered a new ballet titled "The Nutcracker."

In Massachusetts, a Fall River couple named Borden was brutally murdered in their home, and their daughter Lizzie came under suspicion as the murderess. In Washington, Democrat Grover Cleveland was elected to the second of his non-consecutive terms as president.

But in Sevier County, the big news was the harlots that had settled into Copeland Creek and their harshly induced relocation. The White Caps, having achieved their goal and having avoided punishment, interpreted that as their community's tacit approval of their actions. And, indeed, many in the community no doubt harbored sympathy for the group, even if their methods were not strictly lawful.

White Capping is not a concept unique to Sevier County. It appeared in the Midwest, most notably in Indiana, decades before it arrived in Tennessee. It started out as an enforcement mechanism to police community behavior standards without having to adhere to the niceties of due process. Typically, White Caps would disguise themselves with a full-body covering of white fabric with holes cut for the eyes. Though the description may summon images of the Ku Klux Klan, White Caps did not wear the conical—some would say comical—headdress of the Klan. And the White Caps' focus was more on moral behavior than ethnicity, though some White Capping activity did target blacks and Jews, among others.

It is likely that many Sevier Countians who joined the White Caps had no intention of beating anyone with a hickory withe. But it was a secret society, and that kind of organization always attracts an element that wants to belong somewhere, particularly when membership allowed for a quiet knowledge that "I know something you don't know."

So White Cap membership grew rapidly, particularly in the communities of Flat Creek, Catlettsburg, and Pigeon Forge and the area around Sevierville. Prospective inductees were called on to swear a blood oath of secrecy and loyalty. Though the specific wording has been lost to the ages, one traditional account says that the oath was administered with cocked White Cap pistols aimed at

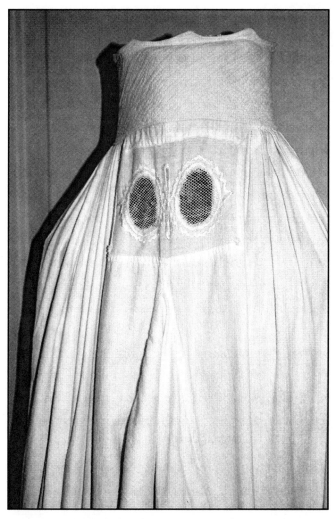

The only authentic White Cap disguise known to have survived is in the possession of the Sevier County Heritage Museum in Sevierville. It is likely most White Cap shrouds were much less stylish than the one in the museum, probably consisting only of white fabric with holes cut out for the eyes.
Photo by Robert Wilson

the new member, who agreed to keep the organization's confidences or be made to receive "100 lashes and leave the county within 10 days or be put to death." Elaborating on that second part, the inductee agreed to "suffer my throat to be cut, my heart to be shot out, and my body to be burned."

All that makes a whuppin' with a hickory limb sound like an ice cream social, but it was apparently pretty effective nonetheless, and as membership grew, those who had taken such an oath began to include men of high stature and financial independence within the community, even government and law enforcement officials and lawyers.

The beatings increased in number as the months went on, with no one prosecuted for what was assault at best and attempted homicide at worst. They occurred almost nightly somewhere in Sevier County, most against women—and sometimes men—accused of "playing pinch and tickle" with someone other than their God-given spouse.

By the light of day, the men responsible for these nighttime atrocities basked in the admiration of their neighbors .

Apparently, little interest was invested in whether the allegations were true or the behavior unlawful. An accusation of infidelity—to one's mate or to the community's standards—was enough to earn you a nocturnal visit from faceless marauders who were prepared to impose their morality based on an extension of the Good Book that was about the length of a hickory withe.

Usually the White Caps, having previously issued their bundle of withes and written warning, would converge on a home in the middle of the night. They customarily beat the door open, dragged the offending individual out into the night, and two or more would hold his or her arms outstretched as their nightclothes were pulled up over their heads from behind. Then the lashes were delivered fiercely by one or more White Caps, most often beating the victim bloody and leaving him or her unconscious, or nearly so, before vanishing into the darkness, their identities still unknown.

Arrests, when they did happen, almost never resulted in convictions, because others in the White Cap organization were always there to provide bail money and legal fees and then to swear that the defendant was somewhere else, doing something else, or there must be some mistake. Furthermore, claims against the attackers were almost impossible to substantiate, because the victim would never see the faces of the attackers inside their White Cap uniform... only the eyes.

The one Sevier County White Cap disguise known to have survived is a fairly sophisticated example, with intricate needlework about the cylindrical head piece, mesh-covered eye holes and a frilly, out-of-character ruffle on the front. It seems that in this case, the wife didn't want her man lashing anybody's back without a properly appointed costume. In all likelihood, however, most White Cap disguises were just sheets with holes cut for vision.

As the White Caps' influence grew, politicians courted their favor and reciprocated by failing to actively pursue their comrades or properly prosecute when they were hauled into court. White Caps were routinely selected for grand juries, making an indictment difficult to come by. And when it did occur, the White Caps would often be aware of it before the indictment was revealed in open court. The same thing applied to trials, where a White Cap in the jury box—and only men could serve on juries—secured at least a hung jury and a mistrial, if not an acquittal.

As a prospective juror was questioned, he might pass his right hand over his cheek, a signal that "I am a White Cap." An attorney would then respond by passing his left hand over his cheek in like manner, signifying his comprehension and answering "So am I." So the White Cap was duly selected. Potential witnesses either perjured themselves in sympathy to the White Caps or were intimidated into doing so. Justice thus subverted, the rest of the court proceedings was all for show, and the White Caps' secrets remained concealed.

•

July nights are sticky in Emert's Cove, and on one of those evenings early on in the White Cap era, a group of the anonymous withe-bearers gathered outside the home of Julia Ramsay, intent on meting out to her a portion of their homegrown justice for transgressions unknown. What the White Caps did not know, however, was that the woman was not alone. What Eli Williamson and Henry Proffitt were doing at her house, no one can say. But they were there, and they were armed.

As was their custom, the White Caps inflicted their initial violence on the cabin door. But that was only the first line of defense. Williamson and Proffitt made up the second line. Unexpectedly, the White Caps were met with gunfire and retreated from what was supposed to be a simple thrashing of a defenseless woman. In the gun battle, one of Williamson's bullets found the leg of attacker Lewallen Sneed. Mountain folk being a clannish bunch, something of a feud quickly developed. The Sneeds were incensed at one of their own being wounded, without regard to the fact he had conspired to commit assault.

A few days after the skirmish, Lewallen Sneed's brother, William, and Houston Romines were seen walking down the road near Williamson's dilapidated log home at the foot of Webb's Mountain on Emert's Cove Road, 14 miles from Sevierville. William Sneed had a rifle.

A narrative of the events has Sneed going to the front door while Romines, wielding a long-blade knife, slinked around back. This time, Williamson was unarmed. Realizing his predicament, Williamson ran to the rear of the house and tried to surrender. Without remorse, Sneed took aim and exacted his revenge.

Williamson died a few hours later, the victim in the first killing directly attributable to the White Caps.

The residents of Emert's Cove had had enough and banded together in opposition to the White Caps under the leadership of John S. Springs, the postmaster for Emert's Cove, who stated for the record:

"Any man or set of men who would go at the dead hours of midnight under the cover of darkness with masks on their faces and drag a poor defenseless woman from her home and lash her back is a base coward and nor worthy of citizenship."

Such a man could also be justifiably deprived of his freedom under the law. But that is not what happened in this case.

William Sneed, it is said, fled across the mountains into North Carolina, and there was no indication by the turn of the century that he ever faced a courtroom in connection with the killing of Eli Williamson.

CHAPTER THREE
The Breedens: Blood Kin

D rawing up the White Caps' organizational chart would have
been a murky undertaking, had it ever been attempted.
Unlike some later organized crime operations, this was a
loose confederation wherein status and rank were likely never entirely clear even to members. Indeed, an organization that performs
its function in the dark is hard to chart even in bright light.

In the absence of a true chain of command, specific titles—for
individuals as well as bands of men—were fluid, except that those
who actively exacted retribution on White Cap victims were called
"raiders," and those who provided bail money, alibis, or legal rep-
resentation were "supporters."

Tradition says that only one man, the main man, had a specific title—actually two. He was the "Chief Mogul" or "High
Cockalorum," A cockalorum is defined as "a self-important little

person." Throwing out the dictionary, if you were that guy in Sevier County, you were SOMEDAMNBODY, respected by many and probably feared by all. But very few actually knew who you were, and that's the way you wanted it.

In the same way that the White Caps' clandestine entry into the court system went a long way toward removing legal liability for the organization's actions, another technical safeguard was added. The group might be White Caps, but they would not call themselves that.

They would adopt the name Grave Yard Hosts, allowing plausible deniability if members were asked, "Are you a White Cap?" The answer was, of course, "No." It was a distinction without a difference, for sure, but perhaps it made them feel better about themselves. They did not have to lie about their affiliation, even if they seemed to have no compunction at all about beating a woman half to death in the middle of the night for tangling up with a married man in the same kind of sheets the White Caps were cutting eyeholes in. A state law passed later in response to Sevier County's White Cap problem would remove the naming distinction, though somewhat belatedly.

Reports vary, but estimates indicate that membership in the White Caps/Grave Yard Hosts ranged from 650 to 1,500. And early on there was little, if any, opposition to the White Caps, organized or otherwise. But that began to change on a May evening in 1893.

•

In its early stages, when dealing with perceived immoral activity between consenting partners, the righteous indignation of the

White Caps turned the "victimless crime" of adultery into one that left people physically maimed or worse. To wit:

Sevier County nights in May can still bring a chill, even if the mountain summer is only a few weeks away. At age 53, Mary Elizabeth Breeden was a widowed mother struggling to provide for herself and four of her children. The eldest, Jesse, 24, was the male presence in the home, and he had three sisters, Mary (also known as Belle), 20, Martha, 18, and Nancy, 11. The word around Jones Cove was that the two older Breeden daughters, both easy on the eyes, were spreading their sweetness a little too indiscriminately around the countryside, either as recreation or as a supplement to the family's meager income. Mary Breeden, however, was not included in the rumors of sexual indiscretion.

Darkness brought a silence to the cove, broken only by the bullfrogs and the katydids and the footsteps outside the windows. The family awoke.

"Jess, Jess, we want to see you," came the cry from one of the horsemen who filled the yard.

Jesse had assumed the mantle of household protector in the absence of a father, and perhaps not remembering in his drowsiness that he had left his pistol at Jesse Robinson's gunsmith shop for repair, he incautiously opened the door without challenging the identity of the caller outside.

Jesse found himself looking at the angry end of a phalanx of firearms. He was inescapably outmanned. Eight men entered the small house, and without much fanfare dragged a screaming Belle Breeden out into the chill in her nightclothes.

There had been no advance warning of this invasion, no bundle of withes with a note attached. But that technicality did not prevent the faceless attackers from carrying out the task at hand. Four of the men took control of Jesse, covering him with their guns. The other four advanced on Belle, stretching out her arms in a crucifixion-style posture, rendering her completely defenseless. The other two pulled her nightgown over her head from the back and began laying on the lashes, this time with knotty black gum withes. Each swing of the branches produced a whistling sound followed by a sickening, fleshy thwack and a painful scream from Belle. One after another, dozens of them, each more violent than the last. The ends of the withes, thin as wool yarn but much more destructive to the skin, lashed and slashed her back, turning it into an agonizing, bloody mosaic. The more she tried to escape, the more severe the beating became. Mary Breeden pleaded with the men, in the name of God, for mercy for her daughter, but the White Caps only invoked the name of the same deity to rebuke her.

"Goddamn you, hush!" came the reply. "It will be your time next."

And then for Belle it was over, except for the hideous pain and a gown stained with blood. She was led, on the edge of unconsciousness, back into the house.

Next on the White Caps' victim list was Martha, who was whipped in like fashion, but a little less severely. This beating was as rhythmic as the first, punctuated by the girl's wailing and her mother's calls for mercy. But mercy was not part of the plan. Not for the girls, and not for their mother.

Mary Breeden was brought to the whipping ground with tears for her daughters still streaming down her face. Now she had to beg mercy for herself. Beseeching her tormentors having proved ineffective, she now hurled invective at them, calling them cowards for their deeds and protesting that her daughters had not done what they were accused of. Maybe that is why her beating was even more savage than the previous two.

As his mother endured her whipping Jesse wept. He was virtually helpless to stop it, though once he attempted to break free of his captors and intervene. But that only caused the bandits to tighten their grip, to the point where one gun barrel nearly touched his face.

In that moment, Jesse heard and recognized the distinctive sound of his own revolver being cocked by one of the attackers. Was it possible Jesse Robinson was one of these White Caps?

The licks and lashes just kept coming until Mary was barely able to cry out any more. At this point, one of the masked nightriders emerged from among his comrades and called a halt to the proceedings. He stepped to the front.

"Don't strike another lick," he commanded. "I know 'is old lady, and she don't deserve treatment like 'is here."

An argument ensued among the bandits on the merits of their mission, and as they were about to resume their tortuous task, Mary Breeden's defender again asserted himself.

"I'll shoot the head off'n the first man who strikes her another lick, if'n I die the next minute."

Maybe it's the bravery or the authoritative leadership. Maybe the strength of the voice or simply the threat that any further loss of Mary Breeden's blood would result in White Cap blood being blended with hers on the ground. In any case, Mary's whipping was over. She was barely conscious and bleeding badly from dozens of open wounds on her back as she was led back into the house.

Her nightgown was soaked in blood, and her long hair had fallen down over her shoulders and become matted in the gore. The Breeden's horrifying ordeal ended with the clip-clop of horse hooves galloping away into the night.

Next morning, as word of the incident spread, anger and sympathy for the Breedens rolled across Jones Cove like a summer storm. Neighbor women arrived to help, as they always did when a family was in crisis. They soaked cloths in warm water to release Mary's hair from the dried blood on her back. They bound her wounds and Belle's and Martha's, too.

The menfolk got details of the attack from Jesse, whose mental anguish was nearly as tangible—and visible—as the welts and gashes on the backs of his sisters and mother. On the ground outside the home were bloody withes with strands of hair still attached.

Jones Cove collectively arose in outrage. Cursing of the White Caps, which prior to this people kept to themselves, now echoed freely through the hills.

Mary Breeden was so badly beaten that she never recovered. She lingered in misery for 3 months before dying.

Around the first of August, a young physician of some skill and increasing influence throughout Sevier County, rode 14 miles to Mary Breeden's home for a house call. Her wounds having been inflicted with something as unclean as a black gum branch, her weakened body was fighting infection on its own, without the aid of medical treatment. After an examination, the doctor told her there was nothing he could do to save her and that her time was short. Mary identified the "Ferguson boys" as being responsible for her battle with death, which she lost on August 4, 1893. Hers was the only whipping that was fatal. Her death gave life to something of a counterinsurgency that formed to fight the White Caps, on their own ground with methods they could understand, and a determination just as resolute as the White Caps' own. And at the head of this opposition was the same man of principle who had been moved by a close-up view of Mary Breeden's death. His title was not as goofy as "Cockalorum." It was a lot more respectable. It was Doctor: Dr. James A. Henderson.

CHAPTER FOUR
A Rising Opposition

A small but scattered outlaw army was still imposing its justice on Sevier County's less-than-respectable women folk as the summer of the hideous Breeden incident faded into autumn and then winter. But also fading was the White Caps' status as the moral conscience and disciplinary authority of the county. A line had been crossed.

It was one thing to kill Eli Williamson. In a mountain-justice sort of way, that could be rationalized based both on the male victim's ability to take care of himself and the fact that in the end, it was a not-uncommon family feud that actually took his life.

But Mary Breeden was a woman. Her family was not feuding with anybody, and these anonymous, cowardly bastards had beaten her to death in horribly brutal fashion. That changed the equation in the minds of some, who now began to lose their sense of humor where the White Caps were concerned. What had started out as an amusing effort to make some whores skedaddle back to Knoxville and to bring some wayward women back into alignment with the King James version had now taken a life without moral justification. There were no allegations that Mary Breeden was making the bedstead squeak with some sweaty hillbilly she wasn't married to. She was just the mother of two pretty girls who may have fooled around some, and there were serious questions as to whether Martha was any more guilty than her mother.

Law enforcement at the time was at best ineffective in combating the White Caps, and most likely was part of the problem. Sheriff George DeLozier, who "served" from 1890 1894, may have even been a passive White Cap himself, a supporter. It is not much of a leap, then, to presume that some of his deputies probably were involved as well.

In a rural county like Sevier, that selective enforcement would amount to a monumental dereliction of duty. But then no one was prepared to call the Sheriff or anyone else to account for fear of becoming the White Caps' next victim. And for that matter, to whom would the whistleblower turn for help?

The Breeden nightmare left a bitter taste in the mouths of residents, many of whom now decided that "maybe this White Cap locomotive had gone off the rails." How far that sentiment extended beyond Jones Cove is hard to say, but it did include the physician who felt powerless to stop Mary Breeden's slow and painful descent toward the grave.

Dr. Henderson was only in his early thirties, but he had gained considerable respect in Sevier County through his medical practice and as a leading thinker and doer in the community. He took Mary Breeden's death as a personal affront.

The doctor was born just a couple of months after the Civil War began and was just short of his twentieth birthday when he married the former Mary Emma Montgomery, who died young. Henderson lived on East Main Street in Sevierville.

Physicians are, by nature, uncomfortable with suffering, which is probably one reason they embark on that career. Mary Breeden's agonizing demise was a source of outrage because it did not have to happen. And though the specific individuals who caused her death might not be identifiable, the umbrella organization they belonged to was. Dr. Henderson made it his quest to thwart the White Caps at every turn, whenever and however possible.

•

Somewhere at its core, there is logic in the concept that a vigilante problem can be addressed by a vigilante solution. That if the law could not or would not rip the sheet off the White Cap, expose his identity, and compel him to face the consequences of his hateful actions, then a robust opposition must do it for them.

After all, the White Caps were born out of the notion that citizens should take care of what law enforcement did not. Dr. Henderson knew that. Thus was born a counterinsurgency known as the Blue Bills, and the good doctor is credited with being the driving force behind it. The Blue Bills had one job and one only—to impede White Cap activities any way possible, even if that required a tug on the trigger. To be sure, if the White Caps were five paces outside the circle of the law, the Blue Bills were three. No, they did not target ordinary folk for minor indiscretions, and their posture was one of defense rather than attack. But in some cases Blue Bill tactics crossed the line to assault and conspiracy. There was blood. There was loss of life. Violence begat violence.

For some period of time almost no one in Sevier County knew whom to trust. The unaligned citizens were afraid of being victimized by the White Caps, who were afraid of being targeted by the Blue Bills, who must have had some trepidation about a law enforcement apparatus that had an incestuous relationship with the enemy. It was a carousel of caution and distrust, with everybody glancing back over his or her shoulder, looking to see who was looking.

The Blue Bills never numbered more than a couple of hundred, it is thought, but no one really knows for sure. On a defensive mission into the countryside, they never attempted to hide their identity. Nor did they have a code of secrecy or some oath to die for the cause. What they did have was intelligence, both the kind attributed to their Cockalorum-equivalent and the kind derived by having double agents in the camp of the adversary.

The Blue Bills likely got their information about planned White Cap escapades the old fashioned way: They bought it, the money presumably coming from the affluent physician. Cockalorums and oaths about having one's heart shot out generated only so much loyalty. A few bucks had a way of dissolving a lot of that.

There is little to indicate where the name "Blue Bill" came from. Some say it was based on a hat they wore, but there is not much to validate that claim. Maybe it was just a name to distinguish them from White Caps. And one of the features of a cap is a bill. But there's no validation for that, either.

Headgear notwithstanding, the Blue Bills, usually outnumbered, seemed to have better information, better firepower, and a stronger will to halt the White Caps than the White Caps had to overcome the resistance and continue with their whuppins'.

The two groups circled each other like angry felines for a time, with armed engagement seeming inevitable.

25

•

Bruce Llewellyn was a White Cap, 24 years and 5 days old, and full of youthful defiance and bravado. Some contingent of his comrades had given notice that they intended to turn their vengeance on Llewellyn's mother. Apparently, membership had no privileges.

Hannah Llewellyn was the mother of seven and had never been married, which would have been common knowledge in the area for at least a couple of decades. But now it became inexplicably important to punish her for her long-ago immoral behavior. Bruce Llewellyn declared that he would see to it that his Mama would suffer no retribution from the White Caps, even if he were among their number.

Multiple White Cap forays to carry out their mission were thwarted by residents and officers, who were obviously being tipped off in advance. That could not be tolerated. The White Caps' focus narrowed to Bruce Llewellyn, because he alone had reason to stop the attack. It had to be him. He had betrayed his oath.

A meeting was called on April 29, 1894, to draw Llewellyn away from home. The route to the meeting took him down Flat Creek Road, 3 miles east of Sevierville, past Millican Grove Church on the north side of the road, across from a thick forest of oak and pine. The night was starless, and Llewellyn took a path through the dark woods southward toward his destination. But along that path, two White Caps were hidden in the undergrowth, probably undisguised because they knew their victim was not going to be able to identify them. A rustling sound in the brush was followed by a shotgun blast that hit Llewellyn in the head and dropped him instantly. His body was found the next day by two small boys who were on their way to a mill.

As Llewellyn was buried in Alder Branch Cemetery 2 days after the killing, people in the area suspected White Cap involvement, but they were disinclined to say it very loudly.

Later information indicated that Llewellyn was not the one who was thwarting the attack on his mother. That did not help Llewellyn much, though. Vigilante justice is often irrevocable in nature.

The Llewellyn killing represented a new level of retribution, a targeted murder. This was not just administering a lashing to a harlot, someone whose societal status was already pretty low and who people probably thought deserved what she got but was allowed to live and leave. On those missions, you didn't have to squint much to see the White Caps actually celebrating their action with whoops and laughter and more than a few slugs of barleycorn. But Llewellyn was a man. He could vote and serve on juries and hold office, and his punishment was just so final.

Trouble is that there was no one to speak up on Llewellyn's behalf. Half the population feared the White Caps as if they were an occupying army, and hundreds of others chose to remain silent . If raising a protest against the organization could get you shot in the head in the dark woods, it was probably smarter to just say nothing.

CHAPTER FIVE
Forewarned But Not Forearmed

L aura Rose opened the door of her Nunn's Cove home one morning, and a bundle of hate and fear fell inside, attached to a crudely handwritten note that addressed her by name and told her, "You better get out of this house in 5 days or we'll give you 75 licks." It was signed by the Sevier County White Caps.

The woman lived there with her children, ages 4 and 6, and the nature of her supposed transgression was not preserved for later generations, nor after the events are there any records of her having lived in Sevier County. Her story was delivered by word of mouth—but not hers and not until a few decades later. But her story sounds about right.

Laura Rose's discovery that morning sent chills of dread down into her very essence. Gathering up the children, she raced to the nearby home of Tom Walker, an affluent farmer and a Blue Bill.

She showed Walker the note, and he swiftly made arrangements for the woman and her children to take sanctuary 12 miles away at a home on Cosby Creek in nearby Cocke County. Walker sent his employee, George Sims, in a wagon to collect the Roses and their belongings and relocate them to Cosby Creek.

That was an all-day task, but when they arrived they were met with another bundle of withes and a note that said, "Laura Rose, you cannot live in this house." It had the same signature as the previous note. Who knew the Rose family was headed there, and how could they have beaten them to the house? The hills had ears, it seemed.

Sims reversed himself and returned to Walker with a fully loaded wagon and a gut full of terror. He told Walker what had happened and basically turned Laura Rose, her children, and the wagon that contained them over to his boss. Though it was now late in the day, Walker escorted them to the nearby home of Campbell Dugan, where they were allowed to spend the night.

The next day there was nowhere else to go except back to their own house, which is where Walker took them. He awakened the next morning to a bundle of withes on his own doorstep with a note warning him not to move the Roses again. Now, Walker was known to be a man whose temper could get hotter'n a blacksmith's forge on an August afternoon. The note triggered a cussin' fit and an oath that he would be ready for any White Cap assault that might come his way. Walker went to Sevierville and bought himself some ammunition and several sticks of dynamite.

A short time later another bundle arrived at the Rose home threatening 150 lashes if Laura Rose did not leave. The White Caps were upping the ante. Walker then moved them to a house in Sevierville that Dr. Henderson offered to Laura and her family.

But when Walker got her to the house, there was another bunch of withes and a warning not to move her and the children in. They were ordering her to leave but giving her no place to go. Now Laura was resigned to getting the beating the White Caps were promising. So she went home.

Every night brought the same fear, and every unidentifiable sound outside the home was a source of terror. Laura Rose began slipping out of her house at dusk and going to a different neighbor's home each night, begging to stay until morning. Then the White Caps caught up with her.

At the home of Frank Keeler one night, a group of about 10 masked men rode into the yard, knocked on the door and bum-rushed those inside, dragging Laura Rose outside. She got her beating.

One man held her arms while another applied the switch. When he tired of his cruel task, he relinquished the withe to a comrade who took up where he left off. Finally, with Laura Rose lying unconscious on the ground, the White Caps rode away.

As always, news of the whipping spread, and Tom Walker now figured they would come for him next for having tried to help. Turned out he was right.

One night shortly after Laura's beating, three men wearing hoods rode into Walker's yard and demanded he come out. He did, but instead of coming out to face the White Caps, he hightailed it out the back door and fled down to the nearby creek and hid under a bridge. That is where he had secured a Winchester shotgun and a battery he planned to use to set off the explosives he had buried in the yard.

As the men entered the house, Walker's wife Anna grabbed an old shotgun and began slugging them with it. As they retreated into the yard, Walker set off the dynamite charges, sending men and

THE EYES OF MIDNIGHT

horses flying in all directions in the darkness. As they tried to flee across the bridge, Walker let go with a shotgun blast that knocked one of the White Caps from his horse.

There is no documentation as to the extent of anyone's wounds that night, but the riders did not exact their revenge on Tom Walker.

•

Dr. Henderson, by this time, was something of a marked man among the White Caps. It was common knowledge that he commanded and financed the Blue Bills, who were just as legally culpable as the White Caps but were facing no threat from the law and no scorn from any segment of the community. Except the White Caps. The word went out among the White Caps that Henderson would feel the withe on his own back. If they could do it to him, logic told them, their supremacy and control would be restored.

But good intelligence from an inside source has a way of trumping the best of battle plans, and so it was in this case, where the Blue Bills knew well ahead of time of the planned assault on Dr. Henderson. When the White Caps converged on the Henderson home, there was already a Blue Bill force in place and ready for action.

The informer rode up to the house with the attackers, but the rode around back on arrival and linked up with the Blue Bills. Henderson was ordered out of his house, but he refused. The shooting started, and White Caps started dropping like teacups in an earthquake, screaming in pain. When the gunfight was over, the Blue Bills stole away into the night, except for a few who remained to stand guard over the Henderson home. It is said that there was a steady stream of wagons and buggies coming and going all night at the battle scene, carting off the dead and wounded.

By the following morning all the casualties had been removed. How many were killed that night—or where law enforcement was during all this—remains a mystery. There are claims that there were multiple suicides reported that next day, each body found with a pistol or shotgun nearby and a note that instructed wives on how to raise their children.

•

In terms of lawlessness, in the late 1800s Sevier County would have compared favorably to towns on the nation's storied frontier. Dodge City's Wild West reputation was always overblown, and Tombstone was in a rocky wilderness that was not even a state yet and still referred to as a territory.

But Tombstone had its silver mines and Dodge City its cattle markets. Sevier County did not have anything like that. And it may have been that lack of a tangible, central commercial engine that allowed the vigilante environment to take root and flourish. There was little to focus on in the way of employment, and for many in the county every day was a study in internal desperation, just trying to make it until tomorrow or springtime or some date in the future that would bring relief. Perhaps White Cap activity was a safety valve for frustration and aggression that was bound up in this day-to-day quest.

None of that, of course, excuses the White Caps' actions—or for that matter the Blue Bills—as a reasonable or justifiable response to the culture in which these individuals found themselves. But it is likely a reflection of the largely unpolished character of a rural mountain enclave like Sevier County.

And the story was not over yet.

CHAPTER SIX
Skirmish at Henderson Springs

I n the time and place that defined the White Caps, Benjamin
Farr might have been called "uppity."

The Civil War was nearly three decades past by 1894, and
African Americans were "free" in the technical and legal sense.
But to claim that they had assumed a full and equal presence in
the American tapestry would be ludicrous. White society in the
South was still a long way from accepting African Americans as
full-fledged American citizens.

However, the Fifteenth Amendment to the U.S. Constitution,
ratified on February 3, 1870, had given black men the right to vote.

As the November off-year election approached, Benjamin Farr,
a black Sevier County resident who was described as mild man-
nered, became vocal in his support for the re-election of John Chiles
Houk as the U.S. Congressman in Tennessee's Second District.

Houk was a Knoxville lawyer who rose to his congressional seat on the death of his father, Representative Leonidas Campbell Houk, in 1890. The younger Houk was re-elected in 1892, but 2 years later he was in a tough Republican primary battle with his father's former law partner, Henry R. Gibson, to retain his seat.

In Sevier County, the African American population was never significant enough to decide an election, let alone one in which Sevier was only one of several counties in the district.

Nevertheless, "Uncle Ben" Farr had been out informally campaigning for Houk in a very public way and making eloquent speeches on the candidate's behalf.

During the run-up to the election, there had been a flurry of beatings in the area, and Farr awoke one evening to find his bed surrounded by White Caps. In apparent response to his political activity, Farr endured not only a nighttime whipping but a humiliating addendum to his punishment. The White Caps forced him onto a stump and ordered him, "Now, damn you, make a speech for Gibson." Fear now trumped Farr's politics, and he made the speech, after which the White Caps retreated.

Sometime during that same period, a woman named Ruth Massey, wife of James Massey and sister-in-law of Dr. Z.D. Massey, attracted the White Caps' glaring eyes for violating her marriage vows. Young and beautiful, she would probably have drawn their gaze even if her virtue had been intact.

One night brought the battering down of the Masseys' door, and both husband and wife were forced outside in their nightclothes. James Massey was held by the White Caps at gunpoint while two others grabbed Ruth Massey's arms and forcibly wrapped them around a tree.

Her gown was lifted over her head, and two intruders applied the lash, in this case, using buggy whips. They started at her feet and worked their way up. It was a brutal and horrific beating that ended after she cried out, "Let me down till I die!" And then she fainted.

She was carried back inside in the belief that she, too, had died from her ordeal. The White Caps fled. Ruth Massey regained consciousness and survived. As always, the neighbors were outraged, but not really to the point of taking any action.

Whether in a bout with his conscience or with a bottle, a White Cap named William Brown let down his guard and told Uncle Ben Farr all about the Massey whipping. He also spilled his innards on the organization's secrets and signs and the White Caps' intention to return to the Massey home to attack James. There was also a plan to converge on the home of one Pink Rauhuff and either burn it down or blow it up.

Farr saw his chance to strike back at the men who had beaten and humiliated him, and he made certain Brown's information found its way to known White Cap opponents in the area.

On an October morning, a man named Elijah Helton came to Sevierville and told the newly elected Sheriff Millard Fillmore Maples about the planned attacks. (Maples had won his post on a platform of combating the White Cap menace.) However, the Sheriff told Helton that he had other pressing matters to attend to and could not personally participate in any law enforcement response to prevent the White Caps' actions. Chancery Court was in session, and his hands were full. So Maples deputized Helton and another man, Mitchell F. Nichols, and instructed them to gather all the sympathizers they could find to prevent the attacks.

On October 25, 1894, Helton and his band gathered at Henderson Springs, a short distance from the mill at Pigeon Forge.

They put together a plan for their evening's work and started for the Massey home.

About a half-mile from Henderson Springs, a bluff overlooks the Little Pigeon River. The road got narrow there, and Helton and Nichols were riding along, accompanied by William A. Henderson, Ash W. Nichols, M.V. Lewellen, John Myers, and Pink Rauhuff.

En route to the Massey home, Henderson, Myers, and Mitchell Nichols got slightly ahead of the others in their party and were the first to encounter four men coming from the other direction who hid their faces behind the brims of their hats as they rode by.

It was suspicious to meet riders there at that time of day, but since they wore no disguises there was no reason to detain them. Seconds later as the men met the rest of the Helton party, angry words interrupted the rhythm of hoof beats. Angry words were followed by pistol shots. The first bullet from a White Cap pistol struck Lewellen in the chest, taking him to the ground.

Helton raised a double-barrel shotgun and emptied it, eliminating two White Caps from the fight. But as he reloaded, a White Cap named James Gibson rushed up and fired twice, both bullets hitting Helton in the head.

Mitchell Nichols and Rauhuff, hearing the gunfire, wheeled their horses around and galloped to the scene, where they found the bodies of Helton and White Cap Isaac Keeble. Labe Latham of the White Cap contingent was also on the cold ground, gasping and moaning. Not knowing if they were in the middle of a crossfire, Rauhuff and Nichols retreated the way they had come. Lewellen, agonizing from his chest wound, headed home.

Mitchell Nichols and William Henderson left the main road, went around the foot of the bluff and forded the river in chest-deep water. All the time they could hear the anguished cries from the killing ground. Latham was crying, "Oh, God I'm shot, and I'm dying. Friends, please come help me."

Mitchell Nichols thought he recognized the moaning voice as that of his brother, Ash. He went to a spot directly across the river from the scene and listened again.

"Oh, Jim, where are you? I am shot and bleeding to death," came the painful plea.

Nichols and Henderson decided the voice did not belong to anyone in their troupe, and they went home.

There, Mitchell Nichols found out that his brother had not returned from the fight, and that rekindled his anguish anew. He paced the floor late into the night, saying, "That poor unfortunate man is dying all alone by the riverside. Surely it must be Ash." When he could not stand it anymore, he returned to a point near the scene to listen. But now there was silence, broken only by the hoot of an owl. Latham was dead, too.

What Mitchell could not know was that Ash was at the home of Rauhuff, fearing that one of the fatalities of the gunfight was Mitchell.

People arriving at the killing scene the next day discovered a sack beneath Keeble's body that contained White Cap masks. Again, tensions rose to the boiling point, and longtime friendships crumbled.

Uncle Ben Farr's friend, William Brown, and two others turned state's evidence in the case, resulting in the arrests of Dan Davis, the alleged leader of the White Cap group, and ten comrades, all charged with the beatings of Ruth Massey and Farr. All went before a justice of the peace and posted bond, but two White Caps were on the grand jury that considered their cases, and no indictments were returned. They all went free. The record appears incomplete on whether James Gibson ever faced charges in the killing of Helton, who was at the time technically a Sheriff's deputy. Lewellen died a year after the battle, the bullet wound to his chest blamed for ultimately causing his death.

•

About a month after the shootout at Henderson Springs, as the evenings were getting chillier and December was only 2 days away, Dr. James Henderson and his second wife, the former Lauretta Murphy, were chatting by their fireside with a neighbor named W.A. Green. It was a Thursday evening.

The sun sets early in late November, and even Main Street in Sevierville was dark and devoid of people. That allowed the man with the shotgun to slip up to the doctor's window without anyone noticing.

He could see the three through the open blinds, their faces a warm orange in the firelight as they talked and chuckled. Slowly he raised his weapon, training it on the doctor. From that distance, it was hard to miss with a shotgun. The man slowly squeezed the trigger.

One second Henderson was talking to his friend, and the next his face was shredded by a shotgun blast that no one saw coming. It was a gruesome scene, the doctor dying almost before he heard the shot.

A jury of inquest, assembled by A.T. Atchley, the county's coroner, readily identified William H. "Bill" Gass as the killer. A warrant was sworn out, and Gass was arrested and jailed under heavy guard.

Dr. Henderson's brother, George Mac Henderson, arrived in Sevierville in a day or so with a casket that he had purchased in

Knoxville. George Henderson publicly disputed the coroner's findings, saying he believed his brother had many enemies and that the murder was likely another White Cap atrocity. A logical conclusion, but not this time.

Bill Gass had eloped to Knoxville with Julia Lillian "Lillie" Maples when the bride was but a16-year-old beauty.

On Friday, November 30, 1894, *Knoxville Journal* breathlessly reported:

> "Last Sunday afternoon a young man of perhaps 35, of medium build, and wearing a light mustache, appeared before the desk of the Hotel Imperial in the city and taking up a pen registered in a bold hand:
>
> Ella Jones, Rutledge
>
> J.A. Henderson, Sevierville
>
> Miss Jones, who had gone to the ladies' parlor, was assigned to Room 64, and Dr. Henderson was given Room 83, which was located on the fourth floor. That night the couple appeared together at supper, and everyone in the dining room was attracted to the young woman's beauty. She appeared to be about 20, with large, lustrous black eyes, arched brows, black hair, and cheeks as red and rosy as a ripe peach. She was of medium height and attired in a plain black dress that perfectly fitted her well rounded figure."

Miss Jones was actually Lillie Maples Gass, who was having an affair with Dr. Henderson. Rumors about his wife's unfaithfulness finally got back to Gass, and he conducted his own investigation. Gass accused his young wife of adultery, and she broke down weeping and admitted her indiscretion with Dr. Henderson at the Hotel Imperial, where a newspaper advertisement showed rooms available for $2.50 a night.

Gass, as a wronged husband, had a motive for the high-profile killing. For his own safety, he was held in a Knoxville jail until his Sevierville trial, at which he was found not guilty. The reasons for the acquittal may have come from sympathy for a man betrayed or because there were White Caps on the jury.

Lillie Maples Gass, by the way, was the only daughter of Sheriff M.F. Maples, who was vehemently opposed to the marriage.

●

The year 1894 also produced one other notable event in the White Cap saga in Sevier County, though its significance would not become widely known for some time: Sheriff Maples hired a new deputy named Tom Davis.

CHAPTER SEVEN
Turning Point

O ld Tom Gibson was an uncomplicated man, a live-and-let-
live sort for whom summers were seasons of hard labor and
winters were to be endured and merely survived. There was
nothing particularly easy about Gibson's existence. He did not have
much, but he seemed to have what he needed, and pretty much all
he asked of life was a peaceful homestead near Sevierville with his
wife and Callie, his daughter. And biscuits on a Sunday morning.
He liked that, too.

Callie had helped make her hard-working father's life a little
easier with her care and support. But she also apparently had an
adventurous side that led her to stray beyond holding hands with
suitors to more intimate activities that Old Tom might have taken
issue with.

On a Saturday evening in April 1895, Gibson was in Sevierville getting some supplies, among them a sack of flour. "I'll have me some biscuits for breakfast Sunday morning," he told those he met. It would not happen.

•

That same Saturday night, a band of White Caps gathered at the home of a man named Jerry Woodsby, who lived in a cabin on property owned by James Catlett, a member of a prominent family in the county. Woodsby had been employed to work on Catlett's farm but had quit for unknown reasons.

The evening stillness was disturbed by a band of White Caps, who surrounded Woodsby's cabin and demanded he come to the door. After Woodsby refused, the bandits battered down the door with a fence rail and dragged him outside, where he received one of the White Caps's fearsome whippings. The beating ended with a stern instruction to go back to work for Catlett or face another, even more brutal, whipping. Woodsby was led back inside bloody and writhing. The White Caps' evening of horror was not over. They proceeded to the humble cabin of Old Tom Gibson a short distance away. Gibson, unlike most others in the county, did not keep a firearm in the house. Apparently, he never needed it or could not afford one.

The White Caps beat down Gibson's door and stepped inside, stating their intention to give Callie Gibson a whipping for her moral shortcomings. Tom Gibson surely must have known how profoundly outmanned he was, and he probably knew that resistance in this instance meant he would never get his Sunday biscuits. Regardless, his fatherly instincts took over, and Old Tom counterattacked with the only weapon he could get his hands on.

Gibson rushed the White Cap leader with a chair while his wife and Callie fled out the back door. The Gibson women would have heard the hateful blast from the double-barrel shotgun as they ran away, in the full knowledge that Old Tom would die and how futile their efforts to alter that outcome would have been. They kept on running in the darkness toward refuge in a neighbor's home.

Old Tom took the shotgun's full fury in his chest, likely killing him before he had time to collapse to the cabin floor. Their mission having gone south in a rapid and deadly fashion, the White Caps namelessly dispersed into the night. Old Tom lay on the cabin floor until morning.

News of Gibson's death did not take long to complete the 2-mile journey to Sevierville, bringing Sheriff Maples, a couple of doctors, a judge, and a bevy of gawkers to the cabin. Something approaching disbelief was the most common reaction to the killing, followed by rising rage that permeated the community.

Maples vowed to run the killers to ground and appealed to William Wynn to loan his bloodhounds to track the murderers. But Wynn refused not only the use of his dogs for the chase, but also declined to participate himself as part of a posse. Whether that raised any alarm in the Sheriff's mind cannot be known, but it would not be the last time that a difference of opinion—to understate the case—would bring Maples and Wynn into conflict.

The incident spurred the Sheriff, a few days after the murder, to request county money to purchase bloodhounds for use in future pursuits. County officials—some of them likely White Caps themselves—hotly debated buying the dogs, but they seemed disinclined to do so until they got a supporting argument from a Sheriff's deputy with a sharp sense of logic and a persuasive tongue.

"This court has just appropriated a large sum of money," Tom

Davis said, "to build a new courthouse. Crime after crime is being committed by a band of White Caps, and to invest a small sum of money in a pair of bloodhounds to run them down, and thus regain the good name of Sevier County, would be of vastly more importance to the county than a new courthouse to try them in."

Davis's argument swung enough votes for the proposal to pass, and the money was appropriated. But shortly thereafter a lawsuit was filed in Chancery Court to block the appropriation. Chancery Court would not meet until nearly 8 months later, and by then the outrage over Old Tom Gibson's murder had died down. The county never bought the bloodhounds, and Gibson's killers never faced a courtroom.

•

The Gibson killing occurred at a pivotal moment in the White Cap chronicle, because it is from this point forward that the organization began to abandon its roots as an enforcement mechanism for Sevier County's morality codes to become not much more than an outlaw band. They ceased to care whether people they attacked were upright or immoral, and that made them even more threatening than before. At least prior to the Gibson killing, one could reasonably expect that if he or she adhered to social mores, the White Caps would leave him or her alone.

But now that began to erode. White Cap bands, in addition to their occasional harlot whuppins', began to stage home invasions for no purpose beyond armed robbery or inter-family disputes. And as often as not, they targeted the aged and those least able to resist. They had lost their theoretical aversion to killing, as evidenced by a case in the middle of August 1896.

Aaron McMahan lived in the splendidly scenic Wears Valley, which is surrounded by mountains and opens up into a valley that is home to the Pigeon River and the appropriately named town of Pigeon Forge. Reports say that the Pigeon Forge area had more White Caps than any other part of Sevier County.

At age 44 McMahan was a successful farmer and had a passel of children, some now old enough to have children of their own. His youngest was still an infant.

McMahan's daughter, Mary, was married to James Clabough, a Sevier County man of modest means but respectability. Of less lofty reputation was Mary, and her virtue was an issue the White Caps felt compelled to address. In typical fashion, they dragged her from her Little Cove home in the night and administered a merciless remedial beating.

The McMahans were, not unexpectedly, both outraged and enraged and let everyone within earshot know it, calling the White Caps cowards and much worse. Quickly identified as being participants in Mary McMahan's attack were Wes Hendricks and Newt Green, first cousins who also lived in Little Cove not far from the Claboughs, 3or 4 miles north of Wears Valley. Aaron McMahan was their uncle; Green and Hendricks were the sons of the brother and sister, respectively, of McMahan's wife, Carline.

Hendricks and Green were hauled into court to face their charges and then were released. The next day McMahan, Clabough, and McMahan's son Amos went to Pigeon Forge in a two-horse wagon loaded with wheat to be milled. While at the mill, a group identified as White Caps encountered the McMahans and Clabough and became engaged in a heated argument over the whipping.

Toward midafternoon, the three men began the arduous trip back to Wears Valley. Four o'clock found them passing through

Little Cove at a point where there are deep woods and hills on the edges of the road. As they rattled down the road, Aaron McMahan heard a noise from the forest and turned to see Hendricks and Green open fire on them. The horses were spooked and began to run. Aaron McMahan, severely wounded, was unable to stop them. Clabough, wounded in the back of the neck and dazed, fell unconscious from the wagon. Amos McMahan took a bullet to the leg.

Passersby managed to halt and calm the horses and took the wounded men to the nearby home of John Myers. As always, members of the surrounding area rushed to the Myers home, as did Dr. Z.D. Massey, who tended all three men's wounds.

Aaron McMahan spent 10 days in agony before dying, but during that time he insisted multiple times that Green and Hendricks fired the bullets that downed all three men. His firm accusation never wavered. Amos McMahan and Clabough both survived their wounds. Others also said they had seen Green and Hendricks in possession of firearms near where the shootings took place. The two were arrested shortly after the shootings by Sheriff Maples and Deputy R.C. McGill and were bound over to a grand jury on high bond on charges of felonious assault. After Aaron McMahan died, the charge was modified to murder, and their bond was revoked. They remained in the Sevier County jail for 7 months, awaiting the March 1897 term of court before going on trial.

Both were convicted of murder, but while they were incarcerated awaiting action on their appeals in the case, Green and Hendricks joined other prisoners in a jailbreak. They were out again.

CHAPTER EIGHT
Trial and Tribulation

I n many ways, Tom Davis ran against the grain of the time and place in which he lived. By adulthood he had some portion of a college education behind him when a sizable segment of Sevier County could not write a grocery list, or for that matter a White Cap note. He was a Democrat in a county so Republican that Election Day was more or less a formality. And he never had much of a sense of humor when it came to the White Caps.

Abraham Lincoln's fateful night at Ford's Theater was 251 days away when Thomas Houston Davis was born, August 7, 1864. On that day Atlanta was broiling under a siege by Union forces commanded by General William Tecumseh Sherman.

The baby boy of J.D. Davis and the former Mary Pickering, daughter of a Sevier County judge, joined a farm family that was flourishing in the heat of both a Tennessee summer and a fading

Civil War. The Davises saw to it that young Tom regularly attended public schools before moving on to a couple of terms at Carson College in Jefferson County and then to Knoxville Business College.

Davis taught school himself briefly but eventually returned to the family farm. At age 23 he married Linnie Adams of Strawberry Plains, and from their wedding day in 1887 they settled into a quiet farm life for 7 years.

For Tom Davis to choose to become a lawman seemed out of character, yet considering how deeply he abhorred the violence in his county and those responsible for it, perhaps it was a sense of community that led him to take the oath of a deputy in 1894. And perhaps it was genetic; his maternal grandfather had been a judge.

Whatever the reason, at some point Davis became one pissed-off, badge-totin' honey badger on the trail of his White Cap prey. The White Caps knew that Davis's smiling face masked a determination to run them to ground in the same way their hoods masked their identities and evil intent. He framed the fight against the White Caps by saying that "the time has come when some man must undertake it, or our county is ruined."

During the course of his several years in law enforcement, Tom Davis would arrest or assist in the arrest of thirty-four White Caps. Included in that number would be Newt Green and Wes Hendricks. Their second-degree murder convictions in the death of Aaron McMahan netted them each a 20-year prison sentence, even though there was convincing evidence—including the victim's dying declaration—that the killing was premeditated and that there were, beyond question, aggravating circumstances.

Whether their punishment was mitigated at all by the presence of White Caps on the jury or within the courtroom apparatus will never be known. And for that matter, what was the revenue source that allowed these two to appeal their convictions to a higher court? It was while that appeal was pending that Hendricks and Green joined a notorious Knox County outlaw named George Thurmer and other prisoners at the Sevier County Jail in overpowering a jailer and taking his keys. Thurmer grabbed the jailer as he handed the prisoner his breakfast and held him as others grabbed the keys. All escaped, and Green and Hendricks fled into the protective hills outside Pigeon Forge. Green and Hendricks were tough and had the indigenous mountain shrewdness that was necessary for survival in the hills. The two spent several months there, staying with White Cap sympathizers in Little Cove but openly walking the roads and working in the fields in the summer of 1897. Sheriff Maples and his men set many a trap for the duo, but advance knowledge of the plans always seemed to thwart their capture.

Rumors of sightings were widespread, but they apparently felt little threat of being taken back into custody. It also became widely known that the desperadoes had been assigned to clean up their own mess by assassinating J.R. Penland, who had prosecuted them; Tom Davis; and Dr. Massey, an unabashed White Cap opponent. But a contact of Massey's alerted the doctor to the plot, and it was foiled.

It was about then that something or somebody led them to the conclusion that it was time to disappear, and they did, just ahead of a deputized posse led by Maples and Davis. That "somebody" may have been Judge Thomas A.R. Nelson, a no-nonsense jurist who had recently begun presiding in a Sevier County court. Nelson had a reputation as a hard-ass without allegiance to any individual or organization in the county and a propensity for dropping the judicial hammer on those found guilty in his courtroom. He had taken over the Sevier County court from Judge W.R. Hicks, a man whose integrity was not being questioned, but whose firmness and courage were suspect.

One July evening Green and Hendricks moseyed into Sevierville, hired a hack, and drove it to Knoxville, where they boarded a train for Texas.

•

At about the same time Green and Hendricks disappeared, so did Tom Davis. For 3 weeks Davis was gone, vanished as far as nearly everyone in Sevier County knew. The truth was he was on the wrong trail, scouring the hills of western North Carolina for two men who had made their escape in exactly the opposite direction. Davis returned home from Carolina with his handcuffs still empty on his belt, and for many weeks afterwards there was little, if any, effort to pursue the fugitives.

Then, following some unknown clue, Davis disappeared again, this time headed for Texas. Only Dr. Massey and Davis's brother-in-law, Andrew Love, knew where Davis was going. Disguised as a book agent, Davis made his way to Paris, Texas, where he connected with local law enforcement and enlisted their help in apprehending Green and Hendricks, but they were not there. Shortly thereafter, Davis received a telegram reading, "Your men at Honey Grove — Z.D. Massey."

Honey Grove, in Fannin County, was a pencil dot of a town in northeast Texas about 30 miles west of Paris. By sunset Davis was in Honey Grove. Again, Davis called upon local lawmen to help with his chase, and they joined the hunt. They scratched the earth all around Honey Grove but could not dig Green and Hendricks out. But they had been seen. The duo again vaporized, hopping a freight train in Honey Grove headed east.

Davis got another telegram: "Your men at New Boston, going by the names of Frank Nolan and Charlie Harrison. — Z.D. Massey." The last passenger train to New Boston had already left Honey Grove by the time Davis got his wire, so he tried to board a freight car himself. A member of the train's crew refused to let Davis ride, telling him he was new to the job because his predecessor was fired for letting two men get on the train to New Boston a few nights earlier. "Where is that man?" Davis asked. He tracked down the now-unemployed fellow, who provided a description of the freight-jumpers that matched that of the fugitives. The trail was getting warmer.

The next morning Davis was at the train depot long before the train to New Boston chugged into town. The deputy boarded the train and rumbled toward the last known location of Green and Hendricks. Davis was met at New Boston by Bowie County Deputy Ed Lynch, but the fugitives were still a couple of steps ahead of their pursuers and had vacated New Boston. Davis and Lynch conducted an intense search of the area but again came up empty. They had vanished without leaving so much as a footprint.

His quest at a dead end, Davis began making preparations to return to East Tennessee. For 8 months Davis had been chasing Green and Hendricks, and all Davis had to show for it was a few more scuffs on his travel bag and a handful of railroad ticket stubs.

About to head home, Davis was waiting at the train station with Deputy Lynch when a cattle trader rode into town. Lynch said to Davis, "There goes a man who has been all over eastern Texas buying cattle. And he never forgets a face." Questioned about Green and Hendricks, the man said he had seen them 11 miles away, headed toward "Indian Territory," which within a decade would become Oklahoma.

Bowie County was in the northeast corner of Texas, at the point where it, Louisiana, and Arkansas all come together. Texarkana shares Bowie County with New Boston. Davis was getting closer.

Faster than the tip of a bullwhip, Davis, Lynch, and the cattle buyer were off in a hack toward their prey. At the Red River they met an old black man and asked him about Green and Hendricks. He told them, "Yassah, boss, I'll tell you. They're right over in that cotton gin right now."

Davis and Lynch crossed the Red River and split up to cover the exits of the cotton gin. Green was the first to be apprehended, Lynch telling him he was wanted in Texarkana. But Green knew better. "Hell, I've heard that tale before. We ain't done nothin' in Texarkana," he said. "I'm guessing, by God, Tom Davis wants us in Tennessee." Green glanced to the side and said, "Hello, Tom. By God, you've got your mustache blacked, but I know you."

Sheriff Tom Davis, center, brings fugitive killers Newt Green, left, and Wes Hendricks back to Sevierville handcuffed together. Davis doggedly tracked Green and Hendricks to Texas and arrested them in connection with the murder of Aaron McMahan.
Photo courtesy of Carroll McMahan

THE EYES OF MIDNIGHT

Hendricks was arrested without much fanfare shortly thereafter. Davis finally got to make use of his handcuffs, chaining Green and Hendricks to each other. On the trip back to New Boston, the captives were heard to sing, "Take me back to Tennessee/There let me live and die."

The Tennessee Supreme Court in November 1898 affirmed the convictions and 20-year sentences of Green and Hendricks in the murder of Aaron McMahan. They are the only two White Caps to spend time in prison for their activities.

There is no explanation on how or from where Dr. Massey was getting his information on Green and Hendricks's movements, which he telegraphed to Davis during the Texas excursion. Somehow though, for much of the chase, he knew where they were before Davis, who was essentially on scene.

Back in Sevier County, the pursuit of Green and Hendricks, dramatic as it was, was overtaken in the public eye by two others, both of them sources of public scorn that was as intense as the crimes themselves. The first was the home invasion robbery of one of the best-loved men in the county, the venerable Andrew Henderson, cheerful as a Christmas tree and known to almost everyone as Old Uncle Andy. With his wife, Sarah, Henderson farmed a fertile riverfront plot in the Henderson Springs area and was known as a plain-speaker, a man of opinions that he was willing to share. One was his disdain for the White Caps.

Couple that with the common belief that Henderson kept a right smart sum of money in his home, and the White Caps had two reasons to target the old man. The second reason probably overrode the first, though.

Born January 13, 1818, Old Uncle Andy had saved his pennies for all of his 78 years and had accumulated more than $2,000,

53

which he kept in a safe in his home in the form of gold. Late on a chilly November evening, the marauders came calling. Someone in the band had knowledge of the old man's habits and knew that he kept his loaded shotgun near his bed at all times. One White Cap broke out a window with the barrel of his own shotgun, so that Old Uncle Andy awoke looking perdition square in the muzzle. Henderson and his wife lay motionless in the bed as other White Caps broke down the door.

Uncle Andy was dragged from his bed and shoved around the room a little before being forced to open the safe. Fear and a possibly fading memory made it difficult to remember the combination, but ultimately he did, and the safe door opened, revealing the shiny gold. The robbers seized it. Old Uncle Andy also usually kept some smooth liquor on hand for his customary morning dram. The bandits knew that, too, and quickly found a two-gallon demijohn of whiskey with the seal still unbroken. With the money and moonshine in hand, the White Caps put a pistol in the old man's face and warned him, "If you ever cheep (reveal) this, your life instead of your gold will pay the penalty."

Their mission complete, the White Caps celebrated their success with gulps of whiskey, whooping and hollering as they rode away from the Henderson home. "White Caps, White Caps!" they shouted, "Hurrah for the White Caps!"

They passed farm after farm, still cheering their victory with alcohol-fueled hoots and laughter until they drew near the Sevierville outskirts. There they slowed, quieted, and dispersed.

Andrew and Sarah Henderson remained in their bed until 10:00 the next morning, afraid that the White Caps were still outside waiting for an opportunity to kill them. Later in the day, Old Uncle Andy's nephew, William Henderson arrived, and the old

THE EYES OF MIDNIGHT

man burst into tears, crying, "Bill, I am ruined! They robbed me of all my gold and left me without a cent!"

A reward was posted in connection with the robbery, but there is no evidence the bandits were ever brought to justice. From that November night through the next couple of months, Old Uncle Andy's mental state deteriorated rapidly, the loss of his life savings seemingly costing him his lucidity. He died broke and broken on February 23, 1897. He was buried in Shiloh Memorial Cemetery. Sarah "Sallie" Pickle Henderson died on July 11, 1916, and was buried next to her husband.

The singular act that would spell doom for the White Caps came a month after Andrew Henderson's robbery.

CHAPTER NINE

Bill and Laura

With the murder of Aaron McMahan, Sevier County's childish amusement with chasing errant women out of the area at the tip of a hickory switch began to mature into a community-wide self-examination: What are we doing? Where is all this headed? Questions began to circulate in the minds of people who valued dignity and justice, and who could see beyond the next harvest season to a future where compassion and human relations had a higher level of refinement and value.

That's not to say that each and every White Cap suddenly abandoned the organization's version of extra-legal corrective measures. Far from it. But support and approval for their tactics among the populace began to erode after the McMahan case, in which a morality-based whuppin' opened the way for a simple retaliatory killing.

Somewhere in there was a just-a-damn-minute moment for many in Sevier County, who now cast side glances at the White Caps when they saw them around town and felt their own sense of justice begin to head in a different direction. Then came the event that pushed anti-White Cap sentiment over the crest of the hill.

•

Bill and Laura Whaley were a young couple whose love for each other far exceeded their material possessions as well as their prospects for an abundant future in Sevier County. Both were the product of the most basic of upbringings, households where the focus was on scratching a tomorrow out of today. Laura McMahan Whaley was the daughter of Blackburn "B.B." McMahan and his wife, Susan Henry McMahan. Theirs was a working-class household west of Sevierville, one of modest means but sound principles. William H. "Bill" Whaley's childhood was even more basic. He was the son of William Thomas Larrimore and Caroline Whaley, who were wed in 1872 in Hamblen County. Census records for 1880 show Larrimore as a resident of the Hamblen County Jail. Perhaps that is why Caroline adopted her maiden name for her two daughters and Bill, who was born in 1877.

Laura Whaley was a year older than Bill, and they were married in December 1892, when they were both still not much more than kids. Three years into their marriage, Bill and Laura Whaley leased a plot of land and a small house from Bob Catlett, the son of a prosperous landowner in Sevier County. It was just a small place where Bill expected to raise a little corn to supplement what he would earn as an employee on Bob Catlett's farm. The lease agreement called for the Whaleys to pay their rent in the form of a portion of Bill's corn crop.

At the time of the lease agreement, the house on the road between Sevierville and Knoxville was occupied by the family of a Walter Maples. When the Whaleys showed up to move into Catlett's house, Maples refused to vacate. Catlett made provision for the Whaleys to take up temporary residence in another cabin he owned until Maples could be evicted.

Bob Catlett was the eldest son of James Catlett, who owned 600 of the best riverfront acres in Sevier County. The younger Catlett had a reputation for unpredictability. There was a wild, reckless streak in him that got broader and deeper when he drank. He had acquired a taste for strong drink while still a youngster, and when he got drunk, his merely overbearing personality became intensely obnoxious, even dangerous; the practical jokes he was known for often crossed the line into downright meanness and cruelty.

Catlett's father facilitated his son's skill at buying and selling superior horse flesh while failing to insist that Bob get an education. It would prove crucial to Bob's future.

By the mid-1890s, Bob Catlett, now married to the former Mary Ann Wade and the father of nine, had reduced his alcohol intake, but when he did drink he was still mean and angry. Catlett had not been an early member of the White Caps, but when he finally was initiated, his focus was less on raising the county's morals and more on achieving his personal, less-lofty goals.

One evening, Catlett and his wife's brother, Bob Wade, came to the house where the Whaleys were staying with a request, though that is not really what it was. Catlett, an illiterate toothache of a man, wanted Laura Whaley to do what he could not—write a note ordering Walter Maples to get out of the house or face a White Cap whipping.

Guided by her sense of rightness, Laura at first declined. But after a warning from Wade that Catlett was hard into the bottle that night and capable of deadly evil, she acceded to the demand. Perhaps it also was that Catlett was holding her husband at gun point.

As Catlett dictated, she wrote: "Walter Maples, if you do not move out of this house in 5 days, the penalty of the White Caps will be visited on you. The time is half up now. — White Caps."

Catlett cursed the 19-year-old woman and swore vengeance on her if she revealed what had happened or shared any White Cap secrets. He then took one of her dresses and cut it into a White Cap disguise.

Catlett and Wade then left for Maples's house, taking Bill Whaley along at gunpoint. They forced Whaley to nail the note to the doorpost of Maples's home before pelting the house with rocks—and even a blast from a shotgun—to make sure Maples did not overlook the warning. Maples and his wife and family shuddered, terrified in their beds, during the incident. Within days, the Maples family fled, and the Whaleys moved in.

Chances are, Laura Whaley was the only one in the room who could read and write on the night Catlett and Wade came calling. Literacy rates were not exceptionally high in rural counties then.

Not only was Laura capable of keeping records, she was meticulous when they pertained to her household finances and her husband's employment records. She knew, as did Bill, that Catlett had not paid him for the work he did on his farm.

In the early spring of 1896, Bill Whaley bought some hogs from Catlett on a bill of sale recorded at the Sevier County Courthouse, with payment to come later. Whaley raised his corn crop at his new home over the summer months. In September, Laura Whaley, now nearing the birth of their first child, calculated that her husband had worked enough unpaid days on the Catlett farm to have satisfied the debt for the hogs. With that knowledge, Bill sold the hogs to pay off other obligations.

•

Late September splashed the East Tennessee hills with a patchwork of warm color that covered the spectrum from sunflower yellow to mousy brown. But the season brought little comfort or delight to the young Whaleys, even as they anticipated the birth of their first baby. Laura Whaley's elder sister, Elizabeth "Lizzie" McMahan Chandler, had come to stay with Laura to help her through childbirth. Lizzie had recently abandoned her husband John, having concluded he was as worthless as goose poop on a garden gate. He was also a White Cap.

When Bob Catlett learned that Bill Whaley had sold the hogs, the volatile side of his nature took control, and he rushed to the Whaley home in a rage. On arrival he found Bill Whaley, who was gathering his corn, and cursed him for having sold the mortgaged hogs and then ordered him to "let the corn alone." Catlett threatened to have Whaley arrested over the hog sale. Whaley attempted to explain that the bill for the hogs was covered by the unpaid days he had worked at Catlett's farm, but Catlett refused to agree and secured a warrant for Whaley's arrest.

The stress of it all was too much for Laura Whaley, who knew that, in the hour when she would need her husband most, he might be arrested for having heeded her counsel to sell the hogs to cover his unpaid wages. She went into premature labor. Mollie Lillard Whaley was born too soon—September 23, 1896—to a mother too young and too fretful about her future.

Rue Catlett, Bob's daughter, was a schoolteacher who possessed all the kindness and compassion that was lacking in her father. Rue came to visit Laura shortly after her new baby was born to congratulate the parents and see the infant Mollie. Rue and Laura were of the same age and temperament, and perhaps that is why Laura felt enough kinship with her to open up about the night Rue's father and Bob Wade forced her to write the Maples note, as well as about the hog deal and the threat to have Bill Whaley arrested.

Rue could apparently touch a soft spot in her father that no one else could reach, and she confronted him about his disagreement with the Whaleys, persuading him to cancel both the debt for the pigs and the arrest warrant for Bill. Later, Bob Catlett went back to the Whaley home to tell them the debt was paid and that the warrant would be canceled. But he also knew that Laura had betrayed White Cap secrets and told her, "For this, you shall die." And Catlett ordered the Whaleys to be off his land by the next day. Believing their landlord to be perfectly capable of carrying out his threat, Bill Whaley bundled up his wife, still weak from childbirth, and his 6-day-old daughter and loaded them into the back of a wagon and relocated them, along with his sister-in-law Lizzie, to a hillside cabin about a half-mile behind the farmhouse of Elkanah M. Wynn, a former Sheriff of Sevier County.

Bill Whaley never got his corn, and the debt for the hogs was never canceled. Based on the theory that a secret known by two people is not really a secret, it was almost inevitable that Laura Whaley's account of the White Cap note would begin to wind its way around the community, particularly after she also told her own mother about it. And the story would travel even faster since it involved a member of one of Sevier County's more prominent families.

Eventually, the story found its way into the courthouse and into the ear of Tom Davis. To him it sounded like the wall of White Cap secrecy beginning to crack, and he seized the opportunity to bring the case before a grand jury. Davis subpoenaed the Whaleys to testify in November 1896.

Bill and Laura, along with Lizzie and the infant Mollie, all came to court, and Laura told the entire story under oath from the witness stand, perhaps the most courageous act of anyone in the White Cap saga other than Tom Davis. Indictments were handed down against Bob Catlett and Bob Wade for the rock-and-buckshot assault on the Maples house, a minor charge in comparison to the McMahan murder, but significant nonetheless.

Lizzie Chandler and Mollie were waiting in the Circuit Court Clerk's office following the court action when Laura Whaley walked in. "Lizzie," she told her sister, "as I came through the hall I met Bob Catlett and Bob Wade. They are going to kill us."

CHAPTER TEN
Vengeance Beyond Measure

B ob Catlett was not the first man to develop such an acute sense of self-importance that he came to believe that the rules were for everybody else, not him. People with extravagant wealth and those in high-level government positions have fallen into the same false confidence for centuries. But often it ends ugly. Whether he felt some measure of legal invincibility in Sevier County or whether he was simply that full of hate, Bob Catlett just could not let go. Yes, he and Bob Wade had done something stupid and gotten in trouble with the law for it. But no one was injured when he tossed some rocks at Walter Maples's house or sprayed it with a little buckshot. And as far as property damage went, well hell, Catlett owned the house. A guilty plea to a charge that he likely could have gotten reduced through his connections at the courthouse and maybe a small fine he certainly could have afforded, and the whole thing might have been over with. But he could not let go. He and Wade were arrested on the Maples charges, made their bond, and were released.

Bob Catlett seethed.

•

Bill and Laura Whaley had little doubt that Bob Catlett meant what he said. He was a man of influence and bluster. He was a bully with a mean streak as wide and long as the French Broad River that rolled by his family home east of Sevierville, and he did not like being crossed, especially by a couple of kids whose entire net worth was probably less than the bond he posted to get out of jail.

November or not, it was too hot in Sevier County for the Whaleys to remain there, and they set their sights on relocating to nearby Anderson County, to the community of Coal Creek, where Laura Whaley is said to have had family. Bill Whaley went first, with the goal of finding work, saving some money, and returning to retrieve his wife, daughter, and sister-in-law.

It took him about a month, but he accomplished his goals, and sometime in December he came back for his family. Immediately on his return, though, he was brought low by a severe case of the grip, as influenza was called then. Upper respiratory infection was a serious killer at that time, often claiming small children when a common cold advanced to untreatable pneumonia. The grip was pneumonia's infectious first cousin.

Bill Whaley was bedridden with fever, a cough, and body aches, and all he could do was wait it out. But more to the point, it delayed his plan to move out of Sevier County and away from Bob Catlett. Catlett's anger had not subsided much since the November grand jury session. It was just lying there deep in his gut, smoldering like a hunk of charcoal deep inside the ashes of a fire that everyone thought was out.

Bob Catlett's social status and his membership in the White Caps meant that if he wanted a job done, he could find somebody to do it. So he began to ask around if this person or that had any interest in a couple of small homicides for hire. The starting price was $50.

He did not get any immediate takers, but he kept asking, and the proposed compensation increased. Finally he asked James Catlett Tipton, a 35-year-old carpenter and blacksmith who had been named for Bob Catlett's father. By then the offer for the job was up to $100.

"J.C.," as Tipton was known in his native Sevier County, had a mid-level education, was well liked, and was thought of as bright and handsome with a little touch of wildness in his nature. He was a fisherman and hunter with a reputation as a dead-on marksman with a pistol or a rifle. Tipton was born August 18, 1861, and at age 23 was working as a carpenter, helping build a new resort hotel known as Seaton's Summer City 8 miles north of Sevierville. It was there he met Mary Seaton, the daughter of the owner of Seaton's Springs and proprietor of the hotel Tipton was helping construct.

Much to the disappointment of the Seatons, their pretty daughter and the carpenter fell in love, and despite their disapproval Mary Seaton and J.C. Tipton got married.

Now, a hundred bucks was a lot of money, enough to get a man through the impending winter and see him through to the following spring. Catlett met Tipton at Fred Emert's store one day and asked to speak to him in a back room, along with Bob Wade. Catlett talked about his vendetta against the Whaleys and that he wanted them "put out of the way" for their testimony, which had gotten him and Wade indicted. Catlett told Tipton that he wanted to make an example of the Whaleys to keep any others from testifying against the White Caps. But Tipton, not bereft of intelligence, declined the offer as others had done before him.

That night, a group of men, including Tipton, Catlett, and Wade, were at a meeting at the Odd Fellows lodge in Pigeon Forge, and as they were riding back to Sevierville they stopped by a turnip patch. Tipton, who had been riding in a buggy with other men, distributed some turnips to them. But when the trip resumed, Catlett prevailed on Wade to ride in the buggy and let Tipton ride his horse so they could talk. Catlett again broached the subject of the paid killings, and again Tipton refused. Catlett then handed an envelope containing four $20 bills and a $20 gold piece to Tipton, telling him the money would be his when the Whaleys were eliminated. Tipton took the envelope home, but the next day he asked J.R. Yett to place the money in the safe at Yett's store. Two days later Tipton retrieved the envelope and gave it back to Catlett, declining once more to kill the Whaleys. In all, Catlett tried more than a dozen times to enlist Tipton into his plot. Catlett told Tipton he was glad he turned the offer down because he thought he could get it done for half the amount he had given him.

Eventually, Tipton did agree to carry out the task—for $50— with Catlett paying any bond or legal fees that might be incurred. Tipton also told Catlett that he had had discussions with a friend and that Pleas Wynn had agreed to go along on the mission.

Pleasant D. "Pleas" Wynn was also known as Shorty for his diminutive stature. "Pleasant" was a name that may have been misplaced on Wynn, who was born in Pigeon Forge in 1869 and lived in adulthood in Sevierville. He possessed the innate shrewdness and cunning of a Sevier County regular, and he did not devote himself much to the three R's. He was active, strong, fast, and competitive, and he never backed down from a fight.

As an adult, married to the former Mary Thomas, Pleas Wynn failed to settle into the role of upstanding citizen and head of household; he was a little too fond of alcohol and games of chance. He never had what could be described as a profession, though he had served at one time as a jailer when his father, Capt. Elkanah M. Wynn, was Sheriff of Sevier County, from 1886 to 1890. The elder Wynn was the owner of the home to which Bill and Laura Whaley moved when Bob Catlett evicted them.

J.C. Tipton and Pleas Wynn, though 8 years apart in age, somehow found common focus on the baseball diamond, along with another youngster who was younger than Tipton but a little older than Wynn: Tom Davis.

•

Both Pleas Wynn and J.C. Tipton knew Bill Whaley "tolerably well," as Wynn put it. "I was barely acquainted with William Whaley," Tipton said, "knew him when I saw him." That was about how well Wynn knew Laura Whaley, but Tipton had never seen her before.

Perhaps that lack of a personal connection made their assignment a little easier. It couldn't have been a lousy 50 bucks that would have to be split two ways. In any event, the conspirators did their best to work it all out ahead of time, with established alibis, precise timing, White Cap masks, and the cover of darkness.

Bob Catlett arranged for his brother Jim to hold the $50 and deliver it to Tipton when the executions were carried out. Three days after Christmas 1896, Bob Catlett harnessed up four horses to take to North Carolina, ostensibly to do some trading but mostly to remove himself from Sevier County.

Pleas Wynn met Catlett at the saddle shop that morning and helped him fix the girth on a saddle, after which Catlett ushered Wynn into a back room and mentioned "putting the Whaleys out of the way." Catlett asked if Wynn had come to an agreement with J.C. Tipton on performing their task, and Wynn said they had. Catlett told him he wanted it done that night.

Catlett left Sevierville about noon with the four horses and an alibi in tow. He stopped for the night 16 miles from Sevierville at the Jones Cove home of George Roland, with whom Catlett sat up late talking.

Wynn and Tipton made it widely known they were going fishing on that cold and moonless night in Hardin's Pool less than a mile south of Sevierville on the west fork of the Little Pigeon River.

At about 5:00 p.m., Wynn dropped by a "blind tiger," a place that sold illegal whiskey, operated by Joe Jenkins on the edge of Sevierville near the east fork of the Little Pigeon. Wynn entered and strode directly to the back room, where he bought a bottle of liquid courage and stowed it in an inside pocket of his ankle-length blue coat.

Wynn asked Jenkins if he could borrow Jenkins's shotgun, but Jenkins told him the gun was already loaned out. In another room, Wynn obtained a pistol. Wynn exited out the back door and worked his way to a ford about a mile down the riverbank, where he met Tipton at the home of Ben Bailey, Tipton's brother-in-law. There Tipton retrieved a shotgun from a tool chest.

The two crossed the river in a boat belonging to Mark McCowan and followed a footpath to the Whaley home. Darkness was no impediment; Wynn knew the path well because it was on his father's farm, and he and his wife had lived in the same house shortly after they married in May 1889.

Wynn and Tipton approached the small cabin quietly and hid in a stable within 20 yards of the house. While huddling in the dark wintry silence, listening to the conversation inside the house, Wynn coughed.

The sound brought John Whaley, Bill's brother, to the cabin door to investigate. With Tipton and Wynn frozen still, John Whaley, pine torch in hand, went to the corn crib and did some nailing on the door of it before going back into the house. A few minutes later John Whaley left his sick brother's house and headed about a quarter-mile home to supper. It was 7:00 p.m., and it was cold.

CHAPTER ELEVEN
Death in the Night

December days are short in Tennessee, and temperatures that are chilly turn downright frigid when darkness overtakes the daylight in late afternoon. There was not much in the Whaley cabin to keep the cold off their noses except a fireplace, nightclothes, and bedcovers. So, with the embers getting low in the hearth, Laura Whaley laid her Mollie—then 3 months and 5 days old—in the arms of the baby's feverish father and joined him under the warming blankets. Lizzie Chandler was in another bed in an opposite corner of the room.

The only sound was the soft crackle of the fire, until the door burst open amid an explosion of fear and splinters. The startled occupants of the cabin bolted upright in their beds, and the women shrieked as both a sense of terror and a rush of freezing winter filled the room. The adults knew that this was likely Bob Catlett making good on his threat, and they could see their end in the fading fireplace light.

Masked and armed, Tipton and Wynn entered the room to find the Whaleys' bed on their right and Lizzie Chandler's on the left. Wynn, wearing his long, blue coat bent to the floor as if to pick something up and his masked slipped away from one side of his face, offering a dimly lit profile to Lizzie Chandler as she trembled in fear.

In a weak voice, Bill Whaley told the men, "If you have come to kill us, we will do anything you say. But spare our lives." But the plea went unanswered; there was no response from the intruders. "Oh, Lord," Laura Whaley screamed, "if you have come to kill us, let me give my little baby to my sister before I die."

Laura kissed the infant and laid her ever-so-gently into Lizzie's embrace. Then she covered their faces with a blanket so they would not have to witness what Laura knew was to come. She moved back across the room to her husband, who had laboriously raised himself and was standing by the bed.

There was no ceremony about the assassins' deed; no words of contempt or vengeance, no blows struck as a tortuous prelude. They just wordlessly did what they came to do. J.C. Tipton pulled the trigger on his double-barrel shotgun, and the first hail of horror tore through Bill Whaley's mouth and face, killing him in a single breath. Laura's last vision was her husband's bloody corpse. The next blast caught her in the temple.

In a matter of seconds it was over. A man twitches his finger twice, and a baby is orphaned in a hideous mist of bone, blood, and brains. And without ever saying a word, Wynn and Tipton backed out the door into the cold and dark. Wynn never fired the Smith & Wesson .44 that was in his pocket.

•

John Whaley was back at the home he shared with his and Bill's mother eating a belly-warming supper when he heard the first shot echoing off the hills.

"What the hell?" he thought. "Is somebody shooting out there... in the darkness and the cold...and at what . . . or whom?"

Then another shot rang out a couple of seconds later. "Wait, is that coming from the direction of Bill's place?"

Without hesitation, John Whaley put his fork down, heaved his heavy coat back on, and lit out again for his brother's cabin a quarter-mile away, bursting through the door at about the moment Lizzie Chandler felt safe enough to emerge from under her bedcovers.

The scene John Whaley encountered was almost too horrifying to be perceived. His brother and sister-in-law—just kids—lay together on the floor in a heap of bloody clothing and unrecognizable faces. An avalanche of "whats" and "what ifs" rushed through his mind in little more time than it took Tipton and Wynn to murder his brother and his wife.

"What happened? What was the motive? What if I had stayed just a little longer? What was that noise I investigated outside?" And most importantly, "Who did this?"

John Whaley rushed outside again and caught sight of a trail through the evening frost, which he followed to a point where someone had crossed the river. There the trail vanished.

After crossing back over the river, Wynn and Tipton quickly retreated to Sevierville, where they split up and set Part B of their plan into action. Tipton returned his shotgun to the tool chest.

Between 8:30 and 9:00, they met up at the courthouse and

returned to the home of Mark McCowan, from whom they had borrowed the boat. They asked McCowan if he wanted to go fishing with them, but he told them he had sick family at his house and declined. It did not really matter; they had made sure someone had seen them around the time of the murders at some distance from the Whaley home.

In truth, they did go fishing, in a manner that not only guaranteed they would catch some fish but would attract some attention to their activity. Wynn and Tipton took McCowan's boat again and pushed out into the river, lit two sticks of dynamite, and tossed them into the water. Their tally for the night: five suckers (carp), a salmon (trout), and two human beings.

Wynn and Tipton returned the boat to McCowan and then buried their masks on the riverbank. Tipton took the salmon and Wynn the suckers, and they returned to Sevierville as the clock in the courthouse struck 10:00 that Monday night. And then they went home.

•

Though no one was appointed to count, it was said that 500 people visited the scene of the Whaley killings. Many saw the disfigured bodies and reflected on the orphaned baby girl and were repulsed by the unbounded wickedness of the act, the cruelty, and the wantonness.

It was just too much for the community to accept. Bill and Laura were just kids, just getting started with their lives and their sweet, innocent baby. Nothing about them signaled that they deserved this. Their murders went infinitely beyond the scope of the White Caps' initial focus of ridding Sevier County of undesirables.

The countywide fear that criticizing the White Caps might bring on their hateful wrath seemed to evaporate almost within hours of the Whaley deaths. There was instant scorn and disdain for the unknown killers and an immediate call for them to be apprehended to face the consequences of their deed. There were open calls for legal retribution, and a righteous avalanche of indignation rolled over the hills. Anti-White Cap sentiment grew by the hour and by the day until such talk became open and unending. Even members of the organization itself turned away in disgust. This was not what most of them had signed up for.

Suddenly, anyone known to have ties to the White Caps came under suspicion, and that was a considerable number. Who did it, and why? And who knew who did it? The speculation rumbled across the county like a two-mule wagon loaded with sawmill slabs.

•

Bob Catlett's $50 bounty did not include killing anyone other than the Whaleys, certainly not a baby. Pleas Wynn and J.C. Tipton knew their victims were not alone in the cabin, but they believed that, since their faces were masked and they never spoke, their identities were secure. And they were for close to a week. But whether a boastful nature got the best of him or alcohol got hold of his tongue, Wynn, never the shiniest coin in anyone's pocket, simply could not keep his actions to himself.

At some point shortly after the murders, Wynn was playing cards with Sam Jenkins and asked him if Jenkins's brother Joe had told him that Wynn had been at the blind tiger the night of the killings.

"Yes," Jenkins said, "he told me all about it."

"Well for God's sake, don't say a word about it," Wynn exclaimed. "By Goddamn, I did kill the Whaleys, and it took a damned sight of nerve to do it. But I got one hundred dollars for the job."

Almost everything in Wynn's statement to Jenkins exaggerated the truth, but he had indeed been part of the conspiracy, and his involvement made him a murderer, even if he did not fire his pistol and only collected $25 "for the job." By week's end, though, the word was getting out about Pleas Wynn's role in the murder plot.

On Friday, New Year's Day, Tom Davis returned to Sevier County from East Bernstadt, Kentucky, where he had taken a fugitive named J.J. Robison into custody. Arising early Saturday, Davis rode to Catlettsburg, where an agitated crowd was still discussing the Whaley murders, which had happened 5 days prior. Davis gathered what information he could and rode straightaway to the murder scene with a promise that he would see justice served in the case.

At the cabin Davis found Lizzie Chandler, still weeping over the loss of her sister and brother-in-law. She recounted the scene of horror to the deputy, along with the information that she had seen the face of one of the killers in profile that night.

"If I ever lay my eyes on that little short man that did the shooting, I will know him," she told Davis. In truth, the man whose face she saw—Pleas Wynn—did not fire the fatal shots. This is a fact she may not have known, because she and the baby Mollie were covered by blankets when Tipton pulled the trigger on his shotgun. Davis, fearing for Lizzie Chandler's safety, ferried her away to his own home for protection. Before sunup on Monday, Davis brought Lizzie Chandler to Sevierville and seated her at an upstairs window at the Mitchell Hotel, overlooking the city center to see if she might spot the man she had seen in the firelight the night of the killings. Hours passed, and more hours. Then at about 11:00 a.m. Lizzie recoiled in horror and pointed to a man she saw saunter by the courthouse.

"That's the very man," she cried, "who killed Sister and Bill Whaley."

CHAPTER TWELVE
Captured and Cuffed

T om Davis was a bushy, broad mustached man endowed with a wiry bundle of determination and energy. He had a receding hairline and close-set, penetrating eyes that peered out from beneath thick, brownish brows. He nearly outran his own shadow double-timing it down the stairs of the Mitchell Hotel to the courthouse lawn, where a seemingly unconcerned Pleas Wynn was meandering among the crowd, many of whom would certainly have heard the rumors of Wynn's participation in the murders of Bill and Laura Whaley a week before.

Lizzie Chandler had only recently come to Sevier County and may not have known Wynn by name, only by his fire-lit profile and possibly by the distinctive long, blue coat he wore. But many of those with deeper roots in the area already had an idea that Wynn was guilty.

During the week since the murders, Lizzie had certainly told her tale of horror to anyone who would listen. And who wouldn't? In addition, discretion never having been one of Pleas Wynn's stronger attributes, he had been bragging about his exploits, not just to Sam Jenkins, but to an acquaintance in Knoxville to whom he remarked:

"Bob Wade and Bob Catlett are not guilty of that murder. They have got the wrong sow by the ear. I blew in two hundred dollars damned easy and fired two shots."

It was only a few seconds after Lizzie Chandler's windowsill identification that Davis had the right sow by the ear. He burst out the lobby door of the hotel and instantly took Wynn into custody, stirring a commotion among those who witnessed the arrest. Minutes later, J.C. Tipton was also nabbed, so unless Wynn implicated his friend within seconds of being taken into custody, suspicion must have also been on hanging on his coattail as well.

Wynn and Tipton were charged with first-degree murder and brought before the justice of the peace that same day in front of a large crowd of onlookers. The defendants were released pending grand jury action. Bob Wade surrendered the next day, January 5, 1897, on charges of being an accessory before the fact in the Whaley murders. Authorities had been alerted by telegram to arrest Bob Catlett—on his horse trading excursion to Asheville, North Carolina—on the same charge as Wade. Davis and Deputy J.E. Keener departed that day to retrieve their prisoner.

Catlett was his usual arrogant self when Deputies Davis and Keener arrived in Asheville, declaring, "I never got into any trouble yet I could not get out of." Davis responded, "Sometimes in a man's life the time comes when a man's money can't save him," and he pulled out a pair of handcuffs. "You don't mean to put them on me, do you?" Catlett asked. "Yes sir," Davis said, "you will wear them back to Tennessee, or you or I one will die in North Carolina."

Neither one died, and Bob Catlett, in what must have been unbearable humiliation, returned in shackles to the county where he had been regarded as an unstoppable force. He and Bob Wade were brought before a justice of the peace on January 16, 1897, in connection with their roles in the murders. Catlett was released, but Wade remained in jail, failing to make his $5,000 bond. Or maybe Wade suspected that Catlett had his eye on eliminating potential witnesses in the case. People like Lizzie Chandler, Tom Davis, and maybe him, too, in which case a jail cell may have been a safer refuge than his own home. Wade must have thought that if Catlett's money could buy the lives of Bill and Laura Whaley, it could purchase his, also.

The arrests of all four of the principals in the Whaley murders did not signal an end to the case, but they did stoke the embers of anger on both sides of the White Cap equation. For those out-raged by the murders, they now had names and faces at which to direct their fury. White Cap members, however, were incensed that their wall of secrecy had been breached and that some of their compatriots—people they had sworn to protect—were now in the clutches of lawmen who had the capability to inflict real damage on the organization.

Meanwhile, Lizzie Chandler, now divorced from the sluggard John Chandler, agreed for some reason to reunite with him and re-sume their lives together in their old home. She climbed up behind him on his horse, ostensibly to go to a friend's house. But when her absence in Sevierville was noticed, Sheriff Maples and Deputy Davis took off in hot pursuit, overtaking them in the mountains just as they were about to cross over into North Carolina. John Chandler was arrested and jailed. Lizzie was spirited away to Knoxville for safety. Catlett had paid Chandler to try to get her out of the county so she could not testify.

Tension in Sevierville was as tight as a banjo string, with everyone wondering what would happen next. Would there be more killings? Would the defendants go into hiding or flee the county? Would a compromised court system somehow thwart the prosecution? Or would there be more arrests? It is likely that nearly everyone in town was a little more cautious about whom they were seen talking to in public.

For his part, Davis was aware that three of the four men implicated in the murders were free and probably had both the capability and inclination to inflict revenge on him, his family, or others. It was said that many people estimated his life expectancy at less than a month and certainly not long enough to present his case against the four to a grand jury.

The Sevier County Court had offered a $500 reward for information that led to the conviction of the Whaley murderers. W.P. Mitchell of Knoxville ponied up $100, and Sheriff Maples and Davis each offered a $50 reward. During this period Davis received a White Cap threat that he would be assassinated unless he resigned from his job as deputy. However, Davis gave the White Caps a figurative poke in their shrouded eye and caught a train to Nashville, where he asked for and received a promise of an additional $500 reward from the state, authorized by Gov. Robert "Fiddlin' Bob" Taylor. On his trip home, Davis stopped in Knoxville for a few days, where he enlisted the assistance of Detectives C.A. Reeder and C.W. McCall to find and interview potential witnesses in the Whaley case who might have fled Sevier County. That connection resulted in several trips between Sevierville and Knoxville for Davis, the routine nature of which resulted in a near-miss on Davis's life.

At that time, small steam-powered paddle wheelers made regular trips between the markets in Knoxville and the docks at Catlettsburg, northeast of Sevierville, hauling freight, goods, and passengers. The French Broad River, which weaves through Sevier from its source in North Carolina, eventually reaches a confluence with the Holston River east of Knoxville, and that is generally considered the head of the Tennessee River, which flows past downtown. When the water was high enough, the shallow-water craft could make it even a little farther up the Little Pigeon River.

On one trip back from Knoxville, Davis was aboard the *Lucile Borden*, an 86-foot boat that could accommodate forty to fifty passengers on its 11-hour trip from Knoxville to Catlettsburg. Passenger fare was $1, and meals ranged from 15 to 25 cents. About halfway through the trip, a similar boat, the *Telephone* came alongside, close enough that a burly black man was able to step aboard the *Lucile Borden*. He began to ask questions about Davis and initiated a dispute with the boat's cook.

But the unnamed black man kept glancing toward the bow of the boat looking for Davis. The deputy, suspicious of the man, circled around and approached the man from the stern. Encountering Davis, the black man gave him a tremendous shove up against a railing and nearly knocked him into the river. Davis tried to draw his pistol with his right hand as he held the man at arm's length with his left. The attacker also tried to draw his side arm, described as a fine Smith & Wesson .44, but the hammer snagged on the lining of his pocket. Davis was able to get his gun out, and suddenly the black man was staring helplessly down its barrel, his face inches away from a hellish death.

Captain James Edmund Newman, owner and skipper of the *Lucile Borden*, disarmed the man and helped Davis secure his prisoner. Davis brought his would-be assassin to Sevierville, but while they were in a court hearing, a second plot coalesced. This time the plan was to accost Davis at Houk Bluff, about a mile and a half south of Sevierville, on the deputy's way home. Davis defeated that conspiracy by simply remaining in town for the night.

•

The year 1897 was the pivotal one for the White Caps. The first few months were consumed by community outrage over the Bill and Laura Whaley murders. But this was also the period during which Tom Davis was hot on the Texas trail of Wes Hendricks and Newt Green for the Aaron McMahan killing and the shootings of McMahan's son and son-in-law.

This was not the kind of attention the White Caps needed or wanted, at least not the ones who still adhered to the initial principle of elevating Sevier County's moral quotient by chasing off the prostitutes and adulteresses, and sometimes their clients and paramours. A sense of lawlessness and paranoia pervaded the county, to the extent that some of Sevier's more influential citizens decided that they needed legislative support to clean up the mess that law enforcement and courts apparently could not. In its March 1897 session, Sevier County's grand jury finally heard the evidence against Wynn, Tipton, Catlett, and Wade, and without much fanfare, all four were indicted for murder or accessory. Wynn and Tipton were immediately arrested again. Wade, according to records, was still in custody.

When Catlett heard that his paid assassins had been arrested again, he fled Sevierville for home, 6 miles east of town. As darkness approached, Davis and Deputy B.A. Rolen also headed out that direction in pursuit. They found the Catlett house surrounded by a high fence and protected by a couple of snarling bulldogs. Still on their mounts, Davis and Rolen called for Catlett to surrender, but there was no response. The deputies got off their horses, drew their side arms, and warily entered the enclosure. The dogs came running at the officers at the gate and circled them a couple of times but did not attack.

At this point, Mary Ann Catlett came to the door, and Davis and Rolen told her Catlett needed to surrender and that if he did not there would be trouble.

"Bob will never come out," she shouted and slammed the door. The deputies then forced the door open, and Catlett shouted from an upstairs room that he would come down to be taken into custody. Bob Catlett arrested and shackled again, the three men began their return trip to Sevierville.

Even before Davis and Rolen could bring in their captive, activity around town quickly reached to nearly the boiling point. In an apparent act of revenge, William Wynn, Pleas Wynn's brother and the man who had refused to allow Sheriff Maples the use of his bloodhounds to track the killers of Old Tom Gibson, assaulted and badly beat J.D. Davis, the respected father of the deputy.

It was learned that the White Caps were planning to intercept Davis and Rolen on their ride back to Sevierville and free Catlett. Friends of the Davises, sensing a possible armed conflict, began gathering all the guns, ammunition, and willing trigger fingers they could find in response to the plan, as well as the growing number of White Caps who were assembling on the courthouse lawn.

Sheriff Maples deputized all the supporters he could find and, leaving a small contingent on guard at the courthouse, rode out to meet Davis, Rolen, and Catlett to escort them back to the jail. They linked up near Catlettsburg. On hearing of the plan, Davis rode off to recruit several more men to the posse. That done, he gave orders to fight to the last, if necessary, and they resumed their journey to Sevierville.

With the area around the courthouse now occupied by White Caps, Davis rode into town at the head of a phalanx of armed men, including Sheriff Maples and Deputy Rolen, who were guarding Catlett. The two groups stared each other down in suspicion and scorn. But the guns remained holstered, and Catlett joined his co-conspirators in jail.

CHAPTER THIRTEEN
New Law, New Judge

Fearful that an armed conflict was imminent, Sevier County officials hustled the defendants into a courtroom that Saturday night for a bond hearing before Judge W.R. Hicks. Davis stood inside the courtroom with a shotgun at the ready in case the standoff were to erupt into violence.

Bloodshed was avoided, but Hicks, whose rulings from the bench were now being questioned as too accommodating to defendants, freed all the suspects in the Whaley murders on bond. No matter how heinous the crime they were accused of, they were out again.

•

To many of Sevier County's political and economic leaders, the normal legal system did not seem capable of re-establishing what the U.S. Constitution calls Domestic Tranquility. There were too few arrests, too few prosecutions, too few convictions—it just was not enough. Some of those who possessed a measure of influence decided that legislative action on two fronts would be required if the county were to be brought under control again.

The first legislative initiative was to pass a new state law designed to specifically address the concept that was at the core of the White Cap phenomenon. It was even called the anti-White Cap law by some, though in the legislation neither that organization nor Grave Yard Hosts nor any other similar organization was referred to by name. The law comprised multiple facets, but the first three were the most pertinent. Section 1 made it a felony to enter into a conspiracy between two or more people to take a human life or to administer corporal punishment—such as a withe whipping—or to burn, destroy. or seize the victim's property. Conviction of such an offense could result in a prison sentence of between 3 and 21 years. That sentence would be in addition to any conviction for the actual assault or killing. Section 2 provided the same punishment for anyone who procured or encouraged another individual to become a part of such a conspiracy.

Section 3 was the one that made the whole law workable, at least in Sevier County. It said that anyone convicted of any act covered in the first two sections would be prohibited from sitting on any trial or grand jury and made it the duty of the court to exclude them. Furthermore, if any suspicion arose about a prospective or seated juror having even participated in any such activity, the court was instructed to immediately look into the matter, calling witnesses if necessary, and to dismiss anyone "shown to be implicated" in the offenses.

Certainly the law covered not just the White Cap organization, but also others. However, its passage in the 1897 legislative session was directly focused on solving Sevier County's White Cap problem, and that law, combined with another, was viewed by county power brokers as a new and powerful cudgel with which to beat back the White Caps.

From the other side of the issue, members of the White Caps, particularly those whose affiliation was common knowledge, had a new fearsome issue to deal with. Now something as simple as jury duty could be dangerous, so White Cap members began to routinely seek exemption from juries, feigning illness or even sending a proxy in their place so the eyes of the court would not turn on them.

Responsibility for enforcing the second piece of legislation fell on the shoulders of Tom Davis.

On the Monday after the Whaley defendants bonded out, Tom Davis, in service to these leaders and his county, boarded a train at Strawberry Plains, headed for Nashville to meet with members of the Tennessee General Assembly. He carried with him a request to realign the criminal court of Sevier County in such a way that Judge Hicks, in whom the county power structure had lost confidence, would no longer preside over White Cap cases. Hicks's honesty or allegiances were not in question so much as his courage and toughness in demanding justice and handing down meaningful sentences.

County leaders prevailed on the legislature to reassign Sevier County's criminal court jurisdiction to the Knoxville district under the hand and gavel of Judge Thomas Amos Rogers Nelson, a much more authoritative jurist who was not known to be beholden to any individual or group nor known to hold back when it came time to confront criminals with their misdeeds and see that they paid the requisite price.

G.W. Pickle, the state's Attorney General who had already successfully defended Tennessee in a border dispute with Virginia, drew up the bill, which was introduced by State Senator Horace Atlee "Mystery" Mann and supported by his fellow Knox County legislator, Senator John C. Houk, a former congressman. Opposition to the court realignment was led by Senator Lucian C. Keeney of Campbell County, who characterized the issue as a personal fight between Davis and Judge Hicks. Judge Nelson, Keeney said, should not be forced on an unwilling population in Sevier County.

Davis, with time in the legislative session running short, returned to Sevier the following Monday without the bill having passed. But it so happened that that Monday was the day the Sevier County legislative body was scheduled to meet. During a 1:00 session, Davis told the court what had transpired in Nashville and asked the members for a resolution in support of the bill that he could show legislators. The resolution passed unanimously, and with that document in hand, Davis mounted his favorite horse and dashed back the 27 miles to Knoxville, where he caught another train to Nashville. The next morning, Tuesday, Davis was on hand when the Tennessee General Assembly was gaveled into session. He presented the unanimous resolution to the legislature, swaying enough votes for passage. Hicks never again presided over court in Sevier County.

•

The anti-White Cap law would not be signed by the governor until the following spring, but Judge Thomas A.R. Nelson, Jr., had a copy of it in his breast pocket when he strode to the bench on his first day presiding over a Sevier County court in July 1897. He was accompanied by Attorney General E. Fred Mynatt.

Nelson was the fifth of 11 children and was named after his father. The elder Nelson was a famed East Tennessee attorney from Roane County, a staunch Unionist during the Civil War. He was elected twice to Congress, but as he was traveling to Washington to begin his second term in 1861, he was captured by Confederate forces in Kentucky and jailed in Richmond, Virginia. He was ordered released by Confederate President Jefferson Davis after promising not to actively oppose the southern government. He also served on the defense team during the impeachment trial of President Andrew Johnson and as a Tennessee Supreme Court justice.

The younger Nelson's legal career is not nearly so well documented, except through his reputation, which was one of toughness. That there was little further biographical data on him could simply be evidence of a legal life that was uncontroversial because it was generally considered straight up and beyond reproach. He had about him an air of dignity and determination that was bound to have given Sevier County's White Caps a full-body shiver, particularly when, after charging his first grand jury in that sweltering July courtroom, he pulled out the copy of the new law and read it to them.

The courtroom was jammed with spectators who wanted to know whether Nelson would be as direct as his reputation indicated. Even in that sweaty room, Nelson seemed cool and deliberate as he read the law, and then, so there would be no misunderstanding, he elaborated on what it meant and the issue it was meant to address. It was the first time in several years that White Caps felt uncomfortable in a Sevier County courtroom. A few White Caps made excuses as to why they could not serve on the grand jury, and others were deposed by the judge, who told them in no uncertain terms they were no more eligible to serve than a horse thief.

If the assembled needed any more proof that Nelson had a low tolerance for nonsense, it came within hours. As the sun set in Sevierville that day, a group of about a dozen young "toughs" decided to engage in a little friendly intimidation, probably incited by some segment of the White Caps and emboldened by that unique brand of fearlessness that comes packaged in a bottle with a cork.

The young men gathered in front of the hotel where Judge Nelson and Attorney General Mynatt were staying and marched back and forth, singing a loud, raucous, and probably off-key rendition of "We will hang Judge Nelson from a sour apple tree..." Sometimes they substituted Mynatt's name for Nelson's.

It was July. The windows were open, so Mynatt and Nelson could not help but hear—and be amused at—the choral performance being staged for their benefit. Nelson summoned Sheriff Maples and had him and his deputies get all the men's names and submit them to Mynatt for indictment on nuisance charges and "general cussedness."

Maples appeared at the courthouse the following Monday in the company of the singers, who were fearful that the judge's wrath was about to come crashing down. Nelson delivered a stern and threatening lecture to the men as they stood silently before him. Nelson placed all of them under bond to appear in court at a later date, but that is pretty much where it ended. No further investigation was conducted, and there was no subsequent court action. But there were no more nighttime concerts outside the hotel, either. The only singing that was to come would be from the witness stand.

Judge Nelson's early action in Sevierville signaled to everyone that the county had undergone a change of direction, particularly in light of the two new laws, which restored credibility to the court system and brought a sense of foreboding to the White Caps. The future of both looked very different.

The rest of the summer and most of the fall in 1897 was a time of evidence gathering for the prosecution against Wynn and Tipton. Sevier County, particularly Sevierville, remained a tense place, but the explosiveness that surrounded the arrests of the four murder defendants subsided. The trials for the deaths of Bill and Laura Whaley were to be separate, though the ones accused of directly causing their deaths were scheduled to be tried together. Their court date was set for November 15.

CHAPTER FOURTEEN
Going Courting

I t is eerily ironic that a brutal double-murder was the catalyst that brought normalcy, whatever that was, back to Sevier County. No one knew it then, but when Bill and Laura Whaley died, so did the White Caps as a viable influence over pretty much anything in the county.

In the outrage that exploded over the killings, the White Caps lost control over law enforcement and the court system, and consequently they lost what gave them their strength—the fear they were able to plant deep in the hearts of average people. Members of the organization, once arrogant and prideful of their affiliation, now strove to suppress any outward connection that might implicate them in the Whaley tragedy.

For 8 months, from the March indictment of Wynn, Tipton, Catlett, and Wade until their trials began in November, Sevier

County waited, whispered, and waited some more for an anticipated new act of White Cap retribution or more indictments. The only certainty about the future was that two local boys whose brashness outweighed their brainpower were about to feel a judge's gavel pounding on their heads in a fashion that had been unthinkable 5 years before.

•

In order to empanel anything close to an impartial jury, Sevier County had to summon 1,200 men from which to choose a 12-man jury to hear the case of the *State of Tennessee v. Pleasant D. Wynn and James Catlett Tipton* on charges of murder in the first degree in the death of Laura McMahan Whaley.

With Judge Thomas A.R. Nelson presiding, the prosecution was handled by an all-star team comprising E.F. Mynatt, J.R. Penland, W.A. Parton, and former U.S. Representative John C. Houk. The defense team was equally stellar in reputation, though it is unclear whether they were on the payroll of someone with cash to spare or simply wanted to be part of the highest profile criminal case virtually in the history of the county. They were Colonel W.J. McSween, George L. Zirkle, and Captain W.M. Mullendore, among others. This cast of luminaries only intensified the public focus on the case, with the lawyers in the courtroom outnumbering the defendants by more than 4 to 1. The case was on the docket for November 15, 1897, 322 days after the Whaleys were killed.

Jury selection consumed 5 days, as prosecutors tried to weed current and former White Caps and their sympathizers out of the jury box. Attorneys on both sides heavily interrogated potential jurors, trying to find men who had not yet formed an opinion on the guilt or innocence of Wynn and Tipton. In Sevier County, that was not easy.

Security was tight at the packed courthouse as the prosecution began calling a parade of witnesses to the stand. Not surprisingly, the prime testimony came from Lizzie Chandler, Laura Whaley's sister and as close to an eyewitness as there was. She recounted to a captivated courtroom how the killers had burst into the Whaley cabin without warning, how Bill Whaley had begged for their lives, how Laura Whaley had kissed her sweet baby Mollie, and how she handed the child over to Lizzie's embrace in the full knowledge that she was about to die an unmerciful death at the hand of someone whose face she could not see.

When Lizzie was asked by prosecutors if she recognized anyone in the courtroom as having been one of the two armed intruders responsible for the death of her sister and brother-in-law, she hesitated as spectators and court officers breathlessly awaited her answer. Finally, her gaze fell on Wynn. The tense silence lingered for a moment, and then she looked at Judge Nelson, who asked her, "Have you found him?"

"Yes," she answered. Attorney General Mynatt asked, "Where is he?" The witness pointed at Wynn and issued a sworn, affirmative identification. "There. He is the man who had the gun on the night of the murder." No equivocation. No reasonable doubt.

It would have been hard for an honest jury to get around that kind of testimony. Lizzie Chandler had placed Pleas Wynn in the room when and where Laura Whaley was shot to death and with a gun in his hand. Little more needed to be said.

Not so, however, in the case of J.C. Tipton. She could not identify him as definitively as she had Wynn. Not having seen his face nor heard his voice, she could only offer a description of the second killer by size and stature. And Laura Whaley, as a protective measure, had pulled bedclothes over Lizzie's face and that of the baby, so that Lizzie had not actually seen that it was Tipton, not Wynn, had fired the fatal shots.

Prosecutors knew that and did not produce much evidence that would convict Tipton. But they did elicit testimony from Tipton on the witness stand that, although he was not complicit in the killings, he had been with Wynn on the night of the murders, and the prosecutors also knew, with that admission, they would get another crack at convicting him at the defendants' second trial, for the murder of Bill Whaley.

The defense team for Laura Whaley's trial did its best to impugn the character of Lizzie Chandler by introducing charges made by her husband John in their divorce case. But that did not carry their case for acquittal very far. Testimony in the trial lasted 4 days, with the courtroom jam-packed every session. That completed, the attorneys prepared their final arguments.

Laura Whaley's parents, Blackburn and Susan McMahan, and Lizzie Chandler and the baby, Mollie Lillard Whaley, all stayed in Sevierville's Snapp Hotel during the trial, as did Prosecutor Mynatt, who occupied a room that adjoined the McMahans'. In the quiet of the evening, with only a wall as thin as a butterfly's wing separating them, Mynatt did not have to strain much to overhear Blackburn McMahan's lengthy and strident prayer for his daughter's soul or to hear the baby's cooing, on the night before he was to offer his final argument.

McMahan reminded the Lord in his own way of Laura's character and sweetness, and in a voice that quivered with emotion he beseeched his God to deliver justice in that Sevierville courtroom for a young mother whose life was always hard and much too brief.

The words and the emotion that passed easily through the hotel wall that night also penetrated Mynatt directly to his core. He was moved by the family's abiding pain and loss and was inspired by their faith and gentleness. The episode, it was said, was the wellspring from which flowed a most eloquent and persuasive appeal to the Sevier County jury to hold the two defendants accountable for their barbarous act. It was an attempt to touch the jurors' sensitivities the way his own had been.

Mynatt, too, recounted for the overcrowded courtroom the burdens of Laura Whaley's life, the circumstances of her death, and he punctuated his oratory with the images that had been imprinted on his mind by Blackburn McMahan's sorrowful prayer. Many a tear had been brushed away by the time Mynatt's address ended at dusk on November 24, the day before Thanksgiving. Judge Nelson gave his charge to the jury by candlelight. The jury retired that night to begin deliberations.

Pleas Wynn had precious little to be thankful for the next day when a verdict of guilty was returned for his role in the death of Laura Whaley. He must have seen that coming; a conviction was inevitable in light of Lizzie Chandler's dramatic courtroom identification, her finger pointing straight at him from the witness stand. He was moved to the jail in Knoxville for safety reasons.

Without a similar accusatory finger point, J.C. Tipton was acquitted but was held on $10,000 bond in preparation for his and Wynn's trial in the killing of Bill Whaley.

As he sat in his cell for the next few months, Wynn must have wondered if he alone would be tagged with responsibility for the murders, all because his White Cap hood had slipped away from the side of his face momentarily in the dim light of the Whaleys' humble hearth. And he had not even fired the fatal shots.

•

As the spring term of Sevier County's Circuit Court approached, the public fervor again began to rise, because Pleas Wynn and J.C. Tipton were to go on trial a second time, for the murder of Bill Whaley. Most everyone knew this would not be the end of the narrative, just one more milepost on the journey. Wynn had been nailed, and now the community returned to see if the proceedings would confirm the common belief that Tipton, who was acquitted of one murder, was in reality just as guilty as the man who had been convicted. The trial began April 5.

The cases for both the prosecution and the defense were essentially restatements of the evidence in the Laura Whaley trial. Lizzie Chandler again was the center of attention with her story of horror and sadness. In addition, the prosecution entered into evidence the prior testimony of J.C. Tipton that he had been in Wynn's company from sunset to midnight on the day of the Whaley murders. With that admission, how could he not have had a role in the slayings?

But it was not an ardent, overheard prayer and the oratory it inspired that would provide the extra-legal drama for this trial. Owen Dickey was the final witness for the prosecution, and he testified that in an encounter on the day of the murders, Pleas Wynn had showed him a handful of bullets and said, "When I go a-fishin', I take these along and kill damn big game."

Wynn's brother William, who had refused Sheriff Maples the use of his bloodhounds and had assaulted the aged father of Deputy Tom Davis, got angry at Owen Dickey. William had been drinking all that spring day, and he was one of those people for whom alcohol was the release valve for the darker side of their personality. When court adjourned, William Wynn confronted Dickey inside the building and began cursing and threatening him and calling him a liar. Responding to the commotion, Sheriff Maples intervened and ordered Wynn out of the courthouse. But then, as the Sheriff was walking back to his office, Wynn and a group of his friends stepped out of a livery stable and turned their curses on him. Badly outnumbered and believing his life was at stake, Maples pulled his revolver and opened fire. The Sheriff fired five times, and four of the bullets found their way into the belly of William Wynn, mortally wounding him.

The Sheriff, now holding a sidearm with an empty cylinder, began to back away from the group and bolted toward the security of his office nearby. But the crowd was able to cut him off and seize him before he could get there. At that instant Deputy Davis arrived on the scene with his own pistol drawn, ready to impose some new thinking on Wynn's companions. Surreptitiously, Davis placed a handful of cartridges in the hand of the Sheriff, who began to reload his weapon. Also arriving on the scene were Detective C.W. McCall and George Thurmer, a notorious Knox County outlaw whom Davis had captured in Kentucky. Thurmer had turned state's evidence and had been providing law enforcement with intelligence on the White Caps for some time.

The confrontation was defused with no further bloodshed, but Sheriff Maples was immediately called to appear before Judge Nelson in connection with the killing of William Wynn. The judge ordered Maples into the custody of the county and instructed Davis to form a strong guard for Maples's protection.

As Davis headed for the jail with his boss-prisoner, Hagan Bailey, who was William Wynn's brother-in-law and Catlett Tipton's nephew, made an attempt to shoot the Sheriff. But before he could get a shot off, Bailey was quickly disarmed and subdued by Detective McCall and then jailed.

Now again, there was so much tension in the Sevier County atmosphere that you could spoon it out of the air.

CHAPTER FIFTEEN
Insurrection Looms

The White Caps typically went about their work under cover of darkness, and that was again the case in the hours after William Wynn was gunned down by Sheriff Maples. A call went out in every direction from Sevierville for all available White Caps to come to town to redress the wrongs being perpetrated on their cohorts by officers of the law and a community that had lost patience with vigilantism.

Maples, still the Sheriff despite being in custody, used a device that did not have a long history in Sevier County at that time to call for help—he telephoned Sheriff Jesse C. Groner of Knox County, Knoxville Police Chief C.A. Reeder, and Blount County Sheriff S.A. Walker. Each responded by dispatching a posse of men at about 9 p.m. to Sevier County. They all linked up at Trundle's Cross Road, 14 miles east of Sevierville near Boyds Creek, and arrived en masse at the courthouse at 4:00 a.m.

Toward sunrise crowds began to gather in the town center, with people on both sides of the White Cap issue abandoning their farm work to stand eyeball-to-eyeball with their opposites. The tense standoff—White Caps facing both their angry neighbors and a beefed-up police presence—lasted hour after hour. But the standoff faded with the day, violence averted by law enforcement's show of force.

One final surreal scene during the murder trial for Bill Whaley emerged as the defense counsel was giving his final argument to the jury and pleading for the acquittal of Wynn and Tipton. As the attorney spoke in the crowded and heavily guarded courtroom—with all the eloquence he could muster—claiming that Pleas Wynn was an innocent man, a funeral cortege bearing the body of Wynn's brother, William, rolled slowly past the open window, providing an eerie backdrop for the speech.

The jury got the case on the afternoon of April 8, 1898, and returned its verdict the next day: Wynn and Tipton were both found guilty of first-degree murder. Appeals to the Tennessee Supreme Court in capital cases are almost routine, and this case was no exception. The appeal was rejected on November 18, 1898, and their sentence—hanging by the neck until dead—was scheduled to be carried out on January 4, 1899. Sheriff Maples was indicted for the killing of William Wynn, despite his claim that it was a case of self-defense.

•

The latter part of the year also brought two other significant events to Sevier County. First, Sheriff Maples, indicted and awaiting trial in the shooting death of William Wynn, was now dealing with the criminal justice system from the other side of the courtroom, pretty much removing any possibility of his re-election. That, plus the recent victory—if that was what it was — over the White Caps opened the campaign up wider than it had been in decades.

In 1898 there were about 4,000 registered voters in Sevier County, all men and comprising about a fifth of the county's population. More than 90 percent of the voters were reliably Republican. The county, like most of East Tennessee, swam against the political stream during the 1800s, opposing secession and staunchly supporting Republican candidates in every election that followed the Civil War. Tom Davis was a lifelong Democrat, making him an outlier and someone probably accustomed to casting his vote for candidates who had not a shred of a chance of winning, if there were a Democrat on the ballot at all. But in the late summer of 1898, a lot of things were changing in Sevier County. One of them was that this Democrat, well-educated and respected by even those with whom he did not agree politically, was recruited to run for Sheriff. His unswerving pursuit of Sevier County's White Caps put a sheen on his reputation that even his political affiliation could not obscure.

Davis's opponent that year was Republican R.H. Shields, who was also respected as a man of honesty and character, who believed in lawfulness and had never been suspected of supporting the White Cap cause. He was, however, also not seen as being as aggressive as Davis. He was rather quiet and unassuming and content to let the White Caps alone if they let him alone.

Sevier County had not ever elected a Democratic Sheriff in anyone's memory, but in August the voters rewarded Tom Davis with that office. Of the roughly 4,000 registered to cast a ballot, 3,530 voted, and Davis won by a margin of 74 votes. In truth, the heavy lifting in the fight against the White Caps was behind him at that point, but the election meant he would preside over the signal event that could be considered the back breaker for the Grave Yard Hosts: the public execution of Wynn and Tipton.

The other outsize event scheduled that fall was the trying of the *State of Tennessee v. William Robert Catlett* on a charge of accessory before the fact of first-degree murder in the death of Bill Whaley. Prosecutors may have sought to try Catlett in Bill Whaley's death first because that was the case in which they had gotten convictions on both Pleas Wynn and J.C. Tipton. The trial was scheduled for November, the same month in which the convictions of Wynn and Tipton were affirmed by the state's highest court.

•

By the final weeks of 1898, there was little doubt in most Sevier County minds that Bob Catlett was the driving force behind the murders of Bill and Laura Whaley, a belief reinforced by the convictions of Wynn and Tipton. Catlett, despite all his resources and broad circle of acquaintanceship, had become a pariah. The public's scorn ran deep and wide, and if assembling a reasonably objective jury for Wynn and Tipton had been difficult, it would be nearly impossible for Catlett. Catlett's attorneys asked Judge Nelson for a change of venue to Hamblen County, a smaller county northeast of Sevier and separated by Jefferson County in between. Nelson granted the motion to move the trial, and it was rescheduled for December 1898 in Morristown.

The state announced its readiness to go to trial at that point, but defense lawyers asked for a delay, saying they could not prepare an adequate case in just 30 days. Of course, the defense, like everyone else involved, knew that by then Wynn and Tipton would have met their fate at the hand of the hangman, preventing two potential witnesses from testifying for the prosecution. Catlett's legal team wanted the trial reset to April 1899 during the next regular term of the Hamblen court.

The new judge in the case had a familiar face; Circuit Judge W.R. Hicks, whose lack of zealousness in rooting out and prosecuting White Caps had cost him his seat on the criminal court bench in Sevier County, would preside over the trial. But Hicks, possibly realizing the threat to his reputation and legacy, called a special term of the court in Hamblen to hear the Catlett case beginning on February 6, 1899.

The word was out by now that both Wynn and Tipton, having accepted the brevity of their futures, were ready to make soul-cleansing confessions about the Whaley killings, which could be key to prosecuting Catlett. The state appealed to outgoing Governor Robert Taylor for a delay in the executions of the killers, which the governor granted. A new date of April 5 was set for the hangings.

When the Catlett case was called in Morristown in February, the defense again begged for a delay, claiming that some of its witnesses could not be present and that it could not go to trial without them. Catlett was represented by W.J. McSween, George L. Zirkle, W.M. Mullendore, and W.S. Dixon of Morristown. Hicks overruled the motion and straightaway began empaneling a jury. Prosecutors G.M. Henderson, J.R. Penland, John B. Holloway of Morristown, and J.C.J. Williams of Knoxville opened the state's case the next morning.

The first witness was Lizzie Chandler, who horrified Hamblen County jurors with the story of the night of the murders, of the physically weak Bill Whaley pleading for his and his wife's lives, of

Laura Whaley handing her infant daughter to Lizzie and covering their faces, of the terrible shotgun blasts and the scene of slaughter that met her eyes when she gained enough courage to reopen them. The story of the wordless, merciless murders—which the woman had recounted with consistency through two trials already—transfixed the Hamblen courtroom. Again she identified Wynn as being one of the intruders and testified that Tipton resembled the other in stature. A couple more witnesses took the stand and were dismissed before the killers themselves were brought into the courtroom.

Wynn's detailed testimony only bolstered Lizzie Chandler's, as he described how he and Tipton had met in Sevierville the night of the murders, how Tipton had retrieved his shotgun from a tool chest, how they had crossed the river and made their way to the Whaley cabin on foot, how while hiding outside a noise they made had brought John Whaley to the door to investigate, and how, after John Whaley had left, he and Tipton donned their White Cap masks and broke open the cabin door.

Wynn quoted the victims' pleadings and told the jury that Tipton had fired the fatal shots, dropping the Whaleys together on the floor. Then he described their retreat to Sevierville.

Wynn said he had known Bob Catlett all his life and had seen him the morning of the murders at a stable in town. After helping Catlett get ready for his horse-trading trip to North Carolina, Wynn said, Catlett called him into a side room and asked if he had talked to J.C. Tipton about accompanying Tipton on the murder mission. Wynn testified he told Catlett he had, and Catlett then told him of the financial terms of the murder-for-hire and said he wanted it done that night after he had left town.

Later, Wynn said, he and Tipton had met with James Catlett, Bob's brother, who told them that Bob Catlett had left $50 with him to be delivered to the killers after the job was done. Wynn said he collected his half of the bounty, $25, from James Catlett 2 days after the murders.

On cross-examination, defense attorneys grilled Wynn about his own trial, at which he had denied any involvement in the murders. Wynn acknowledged that the testimony during his trial was false and designed only to obtain an acquittal on the charges for himself. He testified that at the end of December 1898, at the urging of his wife and a minister of the Gospel, he had decided to give a true account of the killings to the court. The testimony, he said, was given without any promise of leniency for him and in the full knowledge that his execution would proceed on schedule.

Tipton, in a similar bout of guilt and remorse, joined his cohort in confessing his role in the killings and the complicity of Bob Catlett. Tipton told of Catlett's repeated attempts to get him to kill the Whaleys so that they could not implicate Catlett in the rock-and-buckshot assault on Walter Maples's home. Tipton detailed the events leading up to him agreeing to commit the murders and Catlett promising to take care of any bond or legal fees that might arise.

Tipton's account of the day of the murders aligned with Wynn's, and he acknowledged that he was the one who shot both Whaleys in the head. He told of returning to town and going dynamite fishing with Wynn later that night. He said James Catlett had come to Sevierville the next day and paid him the $50 for the killings and that he had given half of it to Wynn. He also said he never harbored any animosity toward either Bill or Laura Whaley.

Tipton's cross-examination mirrored Wynn's, including an admission that the testimony of innocence in his earlier trial had been untrue.

James Catlett testified after Tipton, adamantly denying that he had any role in the murders or that he had paid Tipton any money following the killings. Bob Wade also denied from the witness stand that he had any involvement, and the defense rested. In rebuttal, prosecutors elicited testimony from an assistant cashier at the Bank of Sevierville, named A.T. Marshall, who claimed that James Catlett had withdrawn $50 from the bank on the day after the Whaleys were killed and produced bank books that reflected exactly that.

After 5 days of testimony, Judge Hicks charged the jury on Friday evening, February 10, 1899. Something in all that testimony left a kernel of doubt as hard as a hickory nut—or a silver dollar—in the mind of at least one juror, because at 9:00 the next morning the jury declared itself deadlocked. Judge Hicks called a mistrial and set a new trial for the regular court term beginning April 24, 1899. The case against Bob Wade was *nolle prossed* on March 21, 1899, meaning prosecutors had decided not to pursue the charges against him. The next day, James M. Catlett, Bob's brother, was indicted as an accessory before the fact in the murder of William Whaley.

The new Tennessee governor, Benton McMillin, was asked for another 90-day delay in the executions of Pleas Wynn and J.C. Tipton. He agreed, and in May 1899 the two convicted murderers testified for a second time against Bob Catlett in the death of Bill Whaley. This time, however, Catlett was acquitted, and there would be no further delays for Wynn and Tipton.

CHAPTER SIXTEEN
Last Steps

The ropes that would yank Pleas Wynn and J.C. Tipton into the hereafter had been stretching for months at the Knox County Jail, where the two convicted killers were housed. An unstretched rope can make for a very messy hanging, and since this was to be the first execution in Sevier County in 90 years, officials wanted nothing to go wrong.

On Independence Day 1899, Wynn and Tipton arose early and prepared for a final ride to the Sevier County Courthouse. Their 20-mile journey in a four-seat hack began at 7:15 in the morning. Accompanying the carriage was an escort of 15 deputized men, including Sevier County Sheriff Tom Davis and Knox County Sheriff J.W. Fox, who provided the ropes, tied the nooses, and had black hoods made for the condemned.

Along the route, the entourage made several stops so Wynn

and Tipton could say final goodbyes to friends and acquaintances. They even received ovations at Catlettsburg and Boyds Creek., but there were no attempts to free the men. The troupe arrived at Sevierville at 12:45 p.m., and at 1:00, the convicted killers ate a meal prepared for them at the jail.

An empty gallows awaits its encounter with convicted murderers Pleas Wynn and Jame Catlett "J.C." Tipton. Both were hanged on the courthouse lawn in Sevierville on July 5, 1899, for the murders of Bill and Laura Whaley. Theirs were the last hangings there.
Photo courtesy of Carroll McMahan

Crowds of people began gathering in town the day before the noon hangings, thousands of them. A Knoxville Sentinel headline on the day of the executions, July 5, 1899, proclaimed, "Stroke of twelve sounds death knell."

The next morning, a special breakfast was prepared for the men and was served in the corridors of the jail. Sheriff Fox provided Wynn a razor so that he would not have to meet his Maker with a stubble. Wynn also shaved Tipton.

People gathered in small groups outside the execution enclosure talked in hushed tones. Anticipation began to rise as noon approached, but Sheriff Davis granted the men's request for a delay so that they could have an extra hour with their families.

Hundreds of onlookers line the riverbank and perch on the roof of the jail as Pleas Wynn, convicted in the murders of Bill and Laura Whaley, prepares to be baptized in the Little Pigeon River in Sevierville. An hour later, Wynn was hanged on the courthouse lawn.
Photo courtesy of Carroll McMahan

At that time the Little Pigeon River ran within a few dozen yards of the Sevier County courthouse, and in the defendants' extra hour, Pleas Wynn repented, at least outwardly. Only he and

110

God knew what was truly in his heart, but Wynn requested to be allowed to have a clergyman baptize him before his death. The request was granted. In front of a primitive camera on the far side of the river, Wynn, a minister, and another man who may have been Tom Davis waded into the water in front of hundreds of observers, who watched from the riverbank and the roof of the jail. Wynn was immersed and drawn forth from the water, most certainly hoping his profession of faith was not too late.

Tipton's relationship with God is less clear. He did not join Wynn in baptism that day, possibly because he had already undergone that ritual. Or maybe he simply had not been touched by a providential hand as his co-defendant apparently had.

At 1:00 the bell in the courthouse tower tolled, the death warrants were read in the jail, and the walk to the gallows began, the condemned surrounded by deputies and led by Davis.

A newspaper dispatch—proudly announcing it was delivered "by long-distance telephone" from Sevierville to the Knoxville Journal and Tribune—said the town was eerily quiet in the overcast July humidity as Wynn and Tipton took their final steps up to the platform. They were asked if they had anything else to say, but both indicated their final statements had been written beforehand.

Tipton had admonished, "Tell the young men to keep good company. Bad company has brought me to this." Likewise, Wynn wrote, "Tell the boys to be obedient to their parents." On the gallows, Wynn and Tipton said their final farewells to their families with kisses and had a last word with clergy, and they sang a verse of the hymn "I Need Thee Every Hour." The ministers offered a final prayer for the men's souls just before the hoods were placed on their heads.

John S. Springs, the postmaster for Emert's Cove, who had vocally and publicly chastised the White Caps over their killing of Eli Williamson, placed the nooses around the condemned men's necks and tightened them up.

Published reports said the two seemed resigned to their fate and calm in their demeanor as the moment of their deaths approached. Four physicians were recruited to certify the expiration of the condemned.

Once on the platform, Davis was more or less an observer, with only one more action to take. *"How could it come to this?"* The question rolled over and over in his mind.

It was 1:05 in the afternoon when the White Cap era in Sevier County effectively ended. Davis looked up from the platform deck to his deputy J.E. Keener, who was standing at the opposite corner with his hand on the release lever, and gave him a silent and almost imperceptible nod.

Davis probably did not even see the ugliest part of it from his perch on the gallows platform. With a clunking sound as the trapdoors beneath them swung open, Wynn and Tipton dropped 6 feet down, as far as the ropes would allow. Wynn jerked and quivered and audibly strangled before being pronounced dead 13 minutes later. Tipton's neck was broken, and death came quickly, but the rope also opened up his throat from one jaw to the other. Blood poured from the wound down the front of his clothing. He was certified dead 18 minutes after he dropped through the trapdoor. His death was as hideous as the ones for which he was executed. "Blood Will Have Blood," screamed a newspaper headline over a story detailing the hangings.

The bodies of Wynn and Tipton were cut down from the scaffold and turned over to their families. Both were buried that afternoon, Wynn in Shiloh Memorial Cemetery in Pigeon Forge and Tipton in Roberts Cemetery on Jayell Road.

•

Bob Catlett spent the better part of the next 5 years—and presumably a bag or two of money—trying to escape a fate similar to that of Wynn and Tipton. His brother, James M. Catlett, was also tried as an accessory before the fact in the death of Bill Whaley in Sevier County in the early days of 1900, but on January 5 it ended in a mistrial. He asked for and was granted a change of venue to Blount County on May 16, 1900, and won an acquittal at trial.

It was February 1903 before Bob Catlett faced another courtroom, this time in the death of Laura Whaley. By now, the case against Catlett hinged not on the testimony of Pleas Wynn and J.C. Tipton, but on transcripts of it. As in his first trial in the death of Bill Whaley, a Loudon County jury deadlocked on his guilt or innocence, and he once again obtained a mistrial. His retrial in Laura's murder came on June 8, 1903, and after 5 days of testimony Bob Catlett was at last convicted of accessory before the fact of murder in the first degree.

As he feared, his sentence was the same as that of Wynn and Tipton: hanging until dead. But on October 31, 1903, the Tennessee Supreme Court reversed the conviction. The court ruled that even though the prior testimony of Wynn and Tipton was admissible by transcript, certain restrictions should have been placed on it, and a stenographer's notes should not have been read to the jury. There were also claims that some jurors, who said they had heard of the case and had already formed opinions, were seated over the objections of the defense. Together, the Supreme Court said, that

113

constituted reversible error, and it sent the case back to the lower court.

Bob Catlett was tried again in a Loudon County courtroom beginning on April 4, 1904. After a 5-day trial with restrictions on the transcript testimony of Wynn and Tipton adhered to, he was acquitted. The White Caps era in Sevier County, Tennessee, was over.

EPILOGUE

The White Caps were not much of a factor in Sevier County by the early years of the twentieth century, outside of some lingering suspicions and animosities that were more personal than organizational. The raids stopped, but the wariness between individuals over what may have been done to whom by whom hung on well into the 1950s or 60s.

Most everyone directly involved in White Cap or Blue Bill activity, and even law enforcement or the court system, was dead by then. But family ties being as strong as they are in rural mountain communities, there were many who were only one generation removed and who still did not want anyone talkin' bad about their Pappy or who still held another family responsible for a loss in their own.

That is why the story of the White Cap era has always been a scattershot undertaking and never written down in any cohesive fashion, much of it not written down at all. That could still get a chronicler in a world of hurt even five decades after the White Cap era ended.

The families involved—the Davises, the Catletts, the McMahans, the Whaleys and the Hendersons—would hardly

115

recognize their home county today. They would find their surnames on any number of streets, churches, and other landmarks,
but what was a dusty agricultural county in the 1890s is now popu-
lated by bungee jumps, go-carts, goofy golf, zip lines, chain restau-
rants and hotels, and enough rainbow-colored electric lighting to
have Thomas Edison begging for mercy.

The terrain—the very thing that made Sevier County a remote
island of simplicity during the advent of the Industrial Revolution
and its new complexities—now draws millions of visitors every year
from all parts of the United States and the world. The Great Smoky
Mountains National Park, which now occupies a substantial swath
of Sevier County, attracts as many as 10 million visitors a year, more
than any other national park. Copeland Creek, where the White
Caps story began, is now inside the national park.

The economic spillover from the park, in terms of hotel stays,
meals purchased, and recreation paid for, has resulted in Sevier
County being awash in a flow of money that might dwarf the GDP
of a small nation.

And in truth, there are still those who do not have much en-
thusiasm for any retelling of the White Cap-Blue Bill saga. But
as a part of Sevier County's history, it is what it is, and there is no
pretending it did not happen even if some of the loose ends are never
neatly tied off.

•

And so here is how the story ends: Every indication is that Bob
Catlett got away with murder. There is almost nothing that would
refute that, and there is ample evidence, circumstantial and through
testimony given repeatedly at trial, that he was materially and

financially at the core of a conspiracy that brutally took the lives of two young people, the parents of an infant girl named Mollie. He was even convicted of it once, though that was overturned on a technicality.

Both Pleas Wynn and J.C. Tipton testified to Catlett's involvement, and they had no reason to accuse him if he were not part of the plot and nothing to gain by fabricating it. They had already exhausted their appeals, and their confessions containing the accusations against Catlett were not going to prevent their appointment with the hangman. And their accounts wove perfectly together like lovers' fingers on a Saturday evening stroll. There was also the matter of the $50 bank withdrawal by Catlett's brother, James, the day after the killings, the exact sum of money that Wynn and Tipton said they were paid for the act, the money delivered by James Catlett.

Bob Catlett outlived virtually everyone else on both sides of the White Cap saga. He died November 25, 1940, a resident of Knoxville, at age 84. And even an attempt to get him to open up about it just 3 years before his death got an interested party, whose father was a Blue Bill and who wanted some additional details, a stern warning not to ever open his gate again if he were also interested in continued good health.

Bob Catlett is buried in the two-century-old Shiloh Memorial Cemetery in Pigeon Forge alongside his wife Mary Ann. He outlived her, too. Also buried nearby is Bob Wade, Mary Ann's brother, who was not prosecuted in the Whaley murders.

There is a saying that people should keep their friends close and their enemies even closer. Some have said that Wade's prime concern through all of this was the safety and well-being of his sister, that he knew of Catlett's volatile nature and that by being shoulder-to-shoulder with him Wade thought he could act as not only a shield for Mary Ann, but also as a force to mitigate some of Catlett's darker motivations. But obviously not all.

It can also be speculated that Wade may have been something of an information source for the authorities, if not during the initial phases of the murder investigation then possibly after his own culpability became manifest. That might explain the decision not to prosecute him as part of the conspiracy, even though, according to testimony, he was present at meetings where the murders were discussed before they were carried out, and he alerted no one.

Even without Wade, all the circumstances that immediately followed the Whaley murders and the rapid arrests of Wynn, Tipton, Catlett, and Wade would indicate that someone with intimate knowledge of the murders was feeding information to Sheriff Maples and Deputy Davis. It is easy to see how Wynn could be arrested within days of the killings, based on Lizzie Chandler's positive identification from the hotel window. But what about Tipton, minutes later, and shortly after that, Wade, and the telegram to Asheville authorities to detain Catlett?

Somebody had to know. That was likely George Thurmer, a notorious no-goodnik who had served time in prison for killing a Knoxville policeman. His particular reputation and skill set made him a prime candidate for White Cap inclusion, and Thurmer was indicted along with others in connection with the White Cap robbery of an old pensioner named John Burnett.

Deputy Tom Davis captured Thurmer in Knoxville sometime after the robbery with the help of law enforcement there and brought him back to the Sevierville jail. Thurmer was the prime instigator in the escape that included Wes Hendricks and Newt Green. Thurmer fled to Pineville, Kentucky, where he got employment under the false identity of Charley Wilson helping build the foundation for a railroad trestle. While digging one day he heard a firm order to throw up his hands, and when he looked up he was facing the meaningful end of a loaded .44 in the grasp of a police officer who asked, "Is your name Charley Wilson?"

"Yes, sir," Thurmer answered. "Is your name Pet Thurmer?" the officer then asked. "Yes, sir," came Thurmer's answer. "Is your right name George Thurmer?"

"Yes, sir," Then Thurmer had a question of his own: "Where is Tom Davis?"

By this time, Davis was approaching from the other end of the trestle. The officer pointed toward him and asked Thurmer, "Do you know that man coming yonder?"

"Yes, by God, that's Tom Davis now," Thurmer said. "I dreamed last night he walked right up behind me in a saloon. I grew uneasy and was fixing to leave as soon as pay day come, but it's too late now. I guess I'll go back to Tennessee with Tom.

"He's a good fellow and always pays my fare when we travel together. This is twice he has captured me, and if I ever get out of that old jail again he will never see me anymore. I will go up in a balloon, cut her loose and leave no trace behind."

But back in Sevierville, it is believed that Thurmer began to feed intelligence about White Cap activities to the Sheriff's office.

Now, after the Whaley murders, Pleas Wynn had trouble keeping his mouth shut, and it is possible the details about who all was involved in the case—both killers and co-conspirators—found their way to Thurmer. If he learned from his contacts immediately after the Whaley murders who the perpetrators were, he may have conveyed that to the "good fellow" Davis, facilitating the rapid arrests of Tipton, Catlett, and Wade after the identification of Wynn.

Irrespective of who was informing on the White Caps, providing law enforcement with information on the Whaley murders, Bob Wade's case was *nolle prossed*, and it is unknown how his relationship with Bob Catlett fared after Wynn and Tipton were hanged. What *is* known is that Catlett would have been preoccupied with keeping a noose off his own prosperous neck and probably not interested in any activity that could compromise his defense.

Bob Wade preceded his brother-in-law in death by nearly 20 years, dying on February 28, 1921, just short of his forty-ninth birthday.

•

Thomas Millard Fillmore Maples was approaching the end of his 4 years as Sheriff of Sevier County when he gut-shot an inebriated William Wynn during the trial of Wynn's brother, Pleas, for Bill Whaley's death. Judge Thomas A.R. Nelson had Maples arrested for the shooting, and the Sheriff was ultimately indicted in Wynn's death. Maples claimed the shooting was a case of self-defense because Wynn, who Maples was attempting to take into custody and who was flanked by a group of supporters, was trying to grab the Sheriff's gun and turn it on him. Maples said he had to do what he did. Maples was acquitted on September 7, 1899.

After leaving public office, Maples migrated to Knoxville, where he worked as a deputy U.S. Marshal, a gauger for the Internal Revenue Service, and a police officer. Eventually he became a bouncer and bartender at Lay's Marble City Saloon, owned by James P. Lay, at 135 Central Avenue in Knoxville. Maples briefly ran his own Knoxville establishment called the Arcade Saloon.

Maples bought some property in Sevier County and was planning to relocate when he went to visit Lay at the saloon on April 4, 1907. Some kind of disagreement developed between the men, which erupted into a full-on argument. Lay fired five shots, killing Maples almost instantly. Lay was charged with murder, but those charges were dismissed 8 days later on Lay's claim of self-defense.

Maples was buried in Red Bank Cemetery in Sevier County.

Maples's daughter, the lovely Lillie, the paramour of Dr. J.A. Henderson and the prime reason for his assassination, died at age 82 on December 12, 1955, in Sevier County. She and Bill Gass, who was acquitted of Henderson's murder, had three children.

John and Lizzie Chandler eventually reconciled and resumed their life together. Lizzie died at age 64 in 1937 and John, 10 years later at age 75. They are buried together in Mount Carmel Cemetery in Bradley County.

John S. Springs was so mortified by his having placed the nooses on Pleas Wynn and J.C. Tipton that he spent the rest of his life riddled with guilt, so much so that he refused to allow himself to be interred in a Christian cemetery. His burial place is unknown.

•

Beyond her whipping death on August 4, 1893, not much is known about Mary Elizabeth Breeden's final resting place or that of her husband, Andrew, who preceded her in death. The family's financial circumstances may have prevented the purchase of a cemetery plot, so she and her husband could simply be interred on a family farm somewhere. No death certificate has ever been found for either Mary or Andrew Breeden.

Jesse Breeden, the grown son who was prevented at the point of a gun from intervening in the beatings of two of his sisters and his mother, died June 22, 1942, in Nashville. He and his wife, Sallie, had three children. One of his sisters who were beaten, Mary, 3 years younger than Jesse, died never having been married on October 3, 1946.

•

Thomas Houston Davis served only one 2-year term as Sheriff of Sevier County, leaving office in 1900. He remains the first and last Democrat elected to that office. The final records of him list his occupation as "real estate" and his residence as Knoxville, specifically the Beverly Hills Sanatorium, where he was being treated for tuberculosis. The sanatorium was opened in 1924 under the sponsorship of the Knoxville Civitan Club and was operated by the city. Davis's death certificate indicates he had been under treatment for tuberculosis for 3 years and that a contributing cause of death was "senility."

He died at 9:20 a.m. on August 1, 1930, at age 67, having achieved his goal of defeating the White Caps but without seeing one of his prime targets, Bob Catlett, punished. He was buried in Alder Branch Cemetery in Sevier County.

ACKNOWLEDGMENTS

On some level, *The Eyes of Midnight* can be characterized as a work of history, in that it profiles real events, real people, and a real period in the life of one Tennessee county.

But in another sense, it is no more than a collection of data from multiple sources, independent of each other both in who compiled the information and the time in which they did so. This book stands astride all of those sources and benefits from research, recollection, and data mining done by those whose efforts preceded it. It could not have been completed in any other fashion, and I am grateful to those who plowed this field before me to bring buried facts to the surface.

Ethelred W. Crozier was publisher of Knoxville's City Directory in the days when a book listing the city's phone numbers would have been a truly thin volume. But any pre-Internet print journalist will tell you that the City Directory in any municipality was considered a reliable cross-reference for names, addresses, and — eventually — phone numbers. It was an invaluable source to researchers before me.

Crozier's book, *The White Caps—A History of the Organization in Sevier County,* is actually erroneous on its title page. It was not a history, but a *real-time account* of the period when the White Caps wielded power in the county virtually without fear of opposition. The book was published in 1899, after Pleas Wynn and J.C. Tipton were convicted of the murders of Bill and Laura Whaley but before they were hanged later that year. *The White Caps* identifies Crozier as publisher of the book, but no author is listed. That is likely because there were still enough feelings of betrayal, anxiety, and fear of prosecution then that anyone who admitted to having penned the accounts in Crozier's book might well have become another White Cap victim.

Reading *The White Caps* 115 years later, it is not much of a stretch to conclude that Crozier himself wrote the book. Crozier, who had ready access to typesetting and printing presses, had the capability to turn out a book of this nature in such a short period of time as to rival the self-publishing of a book in today's world. It is entirely possible that Crozier's book was based on verbal accounts by Sheriff Tom Davis. The details given about many of the episodes recounted in the book would have been known only to Davis. But the effusive glorification of Davis as the singular savior of a corrupt county is probably not something the Sheriff would have written about himself.

Presumably to offset the cost of publishing *The White Caps*, Crozier accepted four display advertisements on the final pages, two from farm equipment dealers, one from a hotel, and one from a candy store, all in Knoxville.

In researching *The Eyes of Midnight*, I came across a handful of statements in Crozier's book that just did not dovetail with other data, such as death certificates, census records, and other records. In such cases, I fell back on my journalistic training to make a judgment call on which information logically seemed more plausible and reliable. For instance, if Crozier spelled a name one way but that person's gravestone showed it differently, I used the spelling on the grave marker, assuming that Davis's memory or attention to spelling accuracy, though sound for the most part, were more likely to be mistaken than the actions of a craftsmen being paid by the family of the deceased to get it right for all time.

Most of these discrepancies surfaced as I searched an Internet genealogy database for principal characters in the White Cap saga. The search sometimes—but not always—yielded images of census rolls or other documents that also contained spellings of names or ages that were suspect. Those I reconciled the best I could.

Crozier's book also was the basis for another book published in the 1930s by the locally fabled grocer and politician Cas Walker, about whose veracity and reliability one can obtain varying opinions. Walker's book, *The White Caps of Sevier County*, reprinted swaths of Crozier's book and interspersed between them accounts presumably handed down to him by his father, Tom Walker, a known Blue Bill.

The Blue Bills, integral to the overall chronicle of the White Cap era, were able to thwart isolated White Cap attacks. But the Blue Bills were never able to derail their opponents' activities in any significant way beyond that, and they became pretty much ineffective after their ostensible leader, Dr. J.A. Henderson, was gunned down in his living room by Lillie Maples's jealous husband.

Cas Walker's book—like Crozier's, a first-generation account—probably gives the Blue Bills a higher profile in the era that they merit. And though one can speculate about Walker's motivation, he took that information with him to eternity.

There are three other information sources that deserve credit in this book. One of those is Donald Franklin Paine, a distinguished

Knoxville attorney, lecturer, and author, and a man apparently obsessed with accuracy, integrity, and detail. He was a founding partner of the Paine, Tarwater, & Bickers law firm.

Paine undertook extensive research into the White Cap era, mostly as it pertained to the legalities involved. Paine's work unearthed court transcripts, newspaper clippings, and much more from various archives, and the fruits of his endeavors are catalogued at the University of Tennessee's Hodges Library. Paine died in 2013.

Of incalculable service to the writing of *The Eyes of Midnight* was Carroll McMahan, the county historian of Sevier County, who has also written on and researched the White Cap era. McMahan's institutional knowledge of the county and its background and residents was my literary GPS, steering me in the right direction whenever I asked and not doing so in one of those halting, annoying electronic voices. Carroll McMahan traces his lineage back to both Aaron McMahan and Laura McMahan Whaley.

Thanks also goes to Tim Fisher, a genealogist at Sevierville's King Family Library. His knowledge of county geography and family background was as valuable as his cataloguing of others' research into the White Caps for people like me to delve into.

The Sevier County Courthouse that was funded by the county government during the era of the White Caps is still in use, though it has been modified and added onto over the decades and now has a bronze statue of Dolly Parton on the lawn. But it is no longer subject to periodic flooding as it was then, because in 1967, the Little Pigeon River, which ran just behind the courthouse and in which Pleas Wynn was baptized, was rerouted some distance away.

INDEX

A

Atchley, A.T. 38

B

Bailey, Ben 68
Bailey, Hagan 98
Blind tiger 68, 74
Blue Bills 24, 25, 28, 31, 32, 115, 116, 117, 125
Boyds Creek 100, 109
Breeden, Jesse 122
Breeden, Martha 18, 19, 21, 23
Breeden, Mary 18, 19, 20, 21, 22, 23, 24
Breeden, Mary Elizabeth 18, 121
Breeden, Nancy 18
Brown, William 35, 37

C

Catlett, Bob 57, 58, 60, 61, 62, 63, 64, 65, 67, 68, 70, 74, 78, 79, 83, 103, 105, 106, 107, 113, 114, 116, 117, 120, 122

Catlett, Mary Ann Wade 58, 83, 117, 118
Catlett, Rue 61
Catlettsburg 10, 75, 81, 84, 109
Chandler, Elizabeth "Lizzie" McMahan 60, 62, 70, 71, 72, 75, 77, 78, 79, 94, 95, 96, 97, 104, 105, 118, 121
Chandler, John 79
Chief Mogul/High Cockalorum 16
City Directory xviii, 123
Civil War xviii, 8, 9, 24, 33, 48, 89, 102
Clabough, James 45
Coal Creek, Anderson County 64
Cocke County 29
Copeland Creek 5, 6, 10, 116
Cosby Creek 29
Crozier , Ethelred W. xviii, 123

D

Davis, Dan 37
Davis, J.D. 47, 83
Davis, Linnie Adams 48

Davis, Mary Pickering 47
Davis, Tom 1, 40, 43, 47, 48, 49, 50,
  52, 62, 67, 75, 77, 79, 82, 87,
  97, 102, 108, 111, 118, 119, 124
DeLozier, George 23
Dickey, Owen 97
Dixon, W.S. 104
Dugan, Campbell 29

E

Emert's Cove 4, 5, 14, 15, 112

F

Farr, Benjamin 33
Fisher, Tim 126
Flat Creek 10, 26
Fox, Sheriff J.W. 108

G

Gass, Julia Lillian Maples 39
Gass, William H. "Bill" 24, 25, 28,
  31, 38, 39, 55, 56, 57, 58, 59,
  60, 61, 62, 64, 67, 69, 71, 72,
  73, 76, 77, 79, 82, 88, 91, 92,
  94, 95, 96, 97, 101, 103, 104,
  106, 107, 109, 110, 113, 115,
  116, 117, 120, 121, 124, 125
Gibson, Callie 42
Gibson, Henry R. 34
Gibson, James 36, 38
Gibson, Tom 41, 42, 44, 83
Grave Yard Hosts 17, 86, 103
Green, Newt 45, 48, 52, 82, 118
Green, W.A. 38
Groner, Sheriff Jesse C. 100

H

Helton, Elijah 35
Henderson, Andrew 53, 55
Henderson, Dr. James A. 21
Henderson, George Mac 38
Henderson, G.M. 104
Henderson, Lauretta Murphy 38
Henderson, Sarah 54
Henderson, William A. 36
Hendricks, Wes 45, 48, 52, 82, 118
Hicks, Judge W.R. 50, 85, 104
Holloway, John B. 104
Houk, John Chiles 33
Houk, Representative Leonidas
  Campbell 34

I

Industrial Revolution 3, 116

J

Jefferson County xvii, 48, 103
Jenkins, Joe 68
Jenkins, Sam 74, 78
Jones Cove 18, 20, 21, 23, 68

K

Keeble, Isaac 36
Keeler, Frank 30
Keeney, Senator Lucian C. 88

L

Larrimore, William Thomas 57
Latham, Labe 36, 37
Lewellen, M.V. 36
Little Cove 45, 46, 49
Llewellyn, Bruce 26
Llewellyn, Hannah 26

Love, Andrew 50
Lynch, Deputy Ed 51

M

Mann, State Senator Horace Atlee
    "Mystery" 32, 88
Maples, Sheriff Millard Fillmore 35
Maples, Walter 58, 59, 63, 106
Marshall, A.T. 107
Massey, Dr. Z.D. 34, 46
Massey, James 34
Massey, Ruth 34, 35, 37
McCall, C.W. 80, 98
McCowan, Mark 68, 73
McGill, Deputy R.C. 46
McMahan, Aaron 45, 46, 48, 52, 53,
    56, 82, 126
McMahan, Amos 46
McMahan, Blackburn "B.B." 57
McMahan, Carline 45
McMahan, Carroll 52, 109, 110, 126
McMahan, Mary 45
McMahan, Susan Henry 57
McMillin, Governor Benton 107
McSween, Colonel W.J. 93
Mullendore, W.M. 93, 104
Myers, John 36, 46
Mynatt, Attorney General Fred 89,
    90, 93, 94, 95, 96

N

Nelson, Judge Thomas A.R. 49, 88,
    93, 120
Newman, Captain James
    Edmund 82
Nichols, Ash W. 36
Nichols, Mitchell F. 35

Nunn's Cove 28

P

Paine, Donald Franklin 125
Parton, W.A. 93
Penland, J.R. 49, 93, 104
Pickle, G.W. 88
Pigeon Forge 10, 35, 45, 49, 66,
    113, 117
Proffitt, Henry 14

R

Ramsay, Julia 14
Rauhuff, Pink 35, 36
Reeder, C.A. 80, 100
Robinson, Jesse 18, 20
Roland, George 68
Rolen, B.A. 83
Romines, Houston 14
Rose, Laura 28, 29, 30

S

Seaton, Mary 65
Shields, R.H. 102
Sims, George 29
Sneed, Lewallen 14
Sneed, William 15
Springs, John S. 15, 112, 121

T

Taylor, Governor Robert "Fiddlin'
    Bob" 80
Thurmer, George 49, 98, 118, 119
Tipton, James Catlett 65, 93

W

Wade, Bob 58, 61, 62, 63, 65, 78, 79,
107, 117, 120
Walker, Anna 30
Walker, Cas 125
Walker, Sheriff S.A. 100
Walker, Tom 28, 30, 31, 125
Wears Valley 45
Whaley, Bill 59, 60, 61, 64, 67, 69,
71, 76, 94, 95, 96, 97, 101, 103,
104, 107, 113, 120
Whaley, Caroline 57
Whaley, John 69, 72, 105
Whaley, Laura 57, 58, 59, 60, 61,
62, 64, 67, 70, 71, 77, 79, 82,
91, 92, 94, 95, 96, 97, 103, 105,
106, 109, 110, 113, 124
Whaley, Mollie Lillard 61, 95
The White Caps: A History of the
Organization in Sevier County
xviii

Williams, J.C.J. 104
Williamson, Eli 14, 15, 22, 112
Woodsby, Jerry 42
Wynn, Captain Elkanah M. 61, 67
Wynn, Mary Thomas 67
Wynn, Pleasant D. "Pleas" 66, 67,
68, 74, 75, 77, 78, 83, 94, 96,
97, 101, 103, 107, 108, 109,
110, 113, 117, 119, 120, 121,
124, 126
Wynn, William 43, 83, 97, 98, 100,
101, 120

Y

Yett, J.R. 66

Z

Zirkle, George L. 93, 104